AF585154

for Martin

RED FLOWER BOOKS

Front cover Mahina Mermaid and her Merboy Makoa Tide: Photo by Thor Englestad

Back cover photo by Irina Tennant

Internal design by Valerie Morton and Elizabeth Callan

Layout and printing Graphic Expressions Byron Bay

Title: Blame It on the Rain : Life Around Byron Bay

ISBN(s): 978-0-6483459-0-9

A catalogue record for this book is available from the National Library of Australia.

Blame it on the Rain

Life around Byron Bay

Valerie Morton

Blame it on the Rain

My friend lives in the California desert and moans constantly that it never rains. Across the world, I live in a rainforest near Mullumbimby and whine endlessly that it never stops. It rains so much up here that mushrooms grow in your wardrobe and very large spiders come inside to shelter. You can be standing in the brightest sunshine with a double rainbow ending at your gumboots, watching cane toads breaststroke across the pool and it will be raining. With the forecast having promised, 'mostly fine with a chance of a shower', rain will be bashing against the tin roof of the house so ferociously that you feel like Hitler is attacking you.

Add the deafening croaking of the surrounding frog army (army is actually the proper collective noun for a group of frogs) and conversation is totally impossible, reducing you to sign language or passing notes back and forth. Because you are living in a black spot, you have no mobile coverage and thus are unable to text. Television and radio are rendered mute and the quality of the phone calls from the home line is worse than if you'd been using two tin cans and a piece of string.

Even when the deluge finally stops—sometimes months later—the phone line is so waterlogged that conversations are like Chinese whispers. You get it all wrong, wreck the friendship and kill the deal. It's like the old World War II command that went down the line—'Send reinforcements, we're going to advance.' By the time it reached its destination it had become, 'Send three and four pence, we're going to a dance.'

Bonne
Blackberry
370g e NET

So the Internet and email are my lifeline and salvation, and my tech guy, Big Fred, my saviour, psychiatrist and hero. After years of sorting out various crises, Fred has become a dear friend. He is always there to take my hysterical calls when a day's work suddenly vanishes off the screen into oblivion—or on one horrendous occasion when an entire book disappeared. He patiently answers all my dumb questions and even assures me that I am not his stupidest client. 'Who is?', I ask, amazed.

He tells me that a man called him to complain that the coffee-cup holder on his laptop had broken. Fred assured him that he didn't have a coffee-cup holder on his laptop. 'Of course I bloody do!', the client yelled. 'It's the drawer thing on the bloody side that slides out with a hole in it to put your cup in!' Fred knows he was hearing him right because for once it wasn't even raining.

Who Let The Dogs Out?

Here in northern New South Wales people like to go around barefoot. Even ladies of a certain age in smart frocks forgo footwear. When you see a man in a business suit skateboard past with nothing on his feet but two silver toe rings, it's no surprise that the local shoe shop closed down.

My English Springer Spaniel, Gillie, on the other hand, has a foot fetish and is extremely interested in shoes—especially his owners'. In his world, shoes hold the mystery and meaning of life and can dictate the difference between a good day and a crappy, might-as-well-go-back-to-bed day. Each time I get up from my desk he watches anxiously to see what I am planning to do with my feet. If anything with a high heel appears from my wardrobe (less and less likely nowadays) he picks up his disgusting chewed toy ferret and slinks away to sulk in the bathroom. Sneakers or espadrilles mean a walk around the property, which is pretty good fun—especially if the giant lizard is out and about—but the big excitement is reserved for thongs—because thongs mean THE BEACH.

Many Byron shire beaches have a special section where dogs great and small can fly through the air after frisbees, chase sticks into the ocean and bodysurf back to shore. With everything from bossy little Jack Russells to crazy passive-aggressive Collies, it always amazes that there are rarely any fights. Even mean-looking junkyard dogs smile and act like graduates of anger-management school as they chase each other across the sand and into the waves like frolicking nymphs.

A group of menacing young men swagger their way along the shoreline dressed in the kind of gear you normally wear to a knife fight rather than a beach. As their bad vibes precede them down the sand people get out of their way—in a hurry

Suddenly a Collie crosses the group's path. The Collie's owner nervously calls it back as the biggest and baddest of the bad-asses stops and stares through his Terminator shades at the innocent pooch. Then, as we watch helplessly, a single word comes forth from the mouth of Mr Evil, 'Lassie!'

A woman emerging from the ocean thinks she recognises the dog. He had been found some months before wandering the streets of Byron Bay with a piece of rope around his neck. After being scooped up and rescued, overhauled by the vet, fed up, rehabilitated and made to feel safe, he is now in his furever home and free to race across the sand and into the waves.

The bad boys all gather around for a pat. Lassie licks the hands wearing skull rings and smiles at their cut-off leathers. When you're a dog you never leap to pass judgement. You're too busy leaping for much more useful things, like a frisbee.

Apparently, it's impossible for a person to walk on a beach and feel depressed—or to feel depression's flip side, anger—something to do with the negative ions in the sand. I guess dogs are absorbing them too, right up through their paws. But then dogs are pretty happy most of the time. Why wouldn't they be? They never have to wear shoes and they can wag their tails all they like—big proper tails—not humiliating little stumps. Australia very sensibly passed a law against docking tails and, after the initial hullabaloo, everyone got used to it. Who

knew that Dobermans had long majestic tails to add a final touch of nobility to their streamlined elegance? How wonderful to watch that big Dobie bitch wag that thang. Go girl. If you got it, flaunt it! Woof woof WOOF!

MULLUMBIMBY
I SHOP LOCAL
LOVE'S YOU

Horny Toad

If you happen to be passing a field of cows after a downpour when the sun is coming out, you might see an old van pulling up and its occupants clambering over the fence. You will watch them creep across the paddock whispering and keeping an eye out for any stray farmers.

Stick around and you will see them reappear sometime later, giggling loudly as they leap among the cows, dreadlocks flying. The big animals look on, bored. They are used to strange types invading their pastures and raiding their dung.

For this is magic-mushroom country, home to some of the best gold tops and Blue Meanies this side of anywhere. Nibble as you pick or take them home, fry them up for breakfast with your eggs, make them into tea, or dry them out and enjoy them all year long.

The *Psilocybe cubensis* (gold-top mushroom) species remains illegal in Australia despite promising new studies from the world of psychotherapy, which has recently been hailing psychedelics

such as this as a possible trigger for a 'paradigm shift' in mental-health care.

According to the august *CMAJ (Canadian Medical Association Journal)*, psychedelics, including shrooms, have been used successfully to treat intractable mental-health issues, including post-traumatic stress disorder, addiction, anxiety associated with terminal illness, and depression. As few as a handful of controlled therapeutic sessions—and even just one—have shown huge improvements for a wide range of disorders.

This stuff has not been made up by a bunch of hippies living in a Kombi van. It comes straight from the behavioural pharmacology department of no less than Johns Hopkins University, the holiest of holies. What they would make of that other path to a different reality—frog medicine—I have no idea. Call me old-fashioned but licking a toad to get high is not on my bucket list. I have nothing against cane toads and refuse to run them over, unlike most of my neighbours, on the grounds that they cannot help being cane toads. I concede that they are not things of beauty and find their knobbly warty backs particularly unappealing. Those toad backs are not, however, unappealing to connoisseurs of the toxin contained within these knobbly glands and released when manipulated.

This psychedelic medicine derived from the DMT-rich secretion of the toad is akin to ayahuasca—the new recreational drug du jour—only stronger. DMT (dimethyltryptamine) is, in fact, the dream chemical that naturally occurs in every human brain, which might explain why our dreams are so trippy.

The toad's poison is a complex cocktail of chemicals, the most important being the same toxin found in the deadly foxglove *(Digitalis)* plant. Consumed without the strictest guidance it's lethal. On a less-recreational front, it has been found that cane toads closely resemble Asiatic toads, long and widely used in Chinese medicine. A student at the University of Queensland has shown that the poison from cane toads is very effective at killing cancer cells—prostate-cancer cells, in particular—without harming healthy cells.

With a nice fat grant from Hong Kong, experiments are underway to come up with a delivery system, as the raw chemicals are too toxic for human consumption. They might very well kill you. So the next time some well-meaning soul offers you a toad to lick, you are strongly advised, as Nancy Reagan once advised about all drugs, to, 'Just say no'. Come to think of it, the former First Lady looked like she might have licked a toad or two late at night in the White House kitchen.

In The Garden

For over a century the endearing little Mullumbimby train station sat on the Murwillumbah line, ferrying travellers up from Sydney and locals between the towns of the Northern Rivers, freeing them from the servitude of the long and winding roads. Since 2004 this country treasure has been sitting forlorn and empty. In its wisdom, the NSW government terminated travel by rail, an act of folly only bureaucrats with comfortable cars and no romance in their hearts could dream up. Abandoned and crying out for some TLC, the 1890's landmark was attracting the wrong sort of attention. Unimaginative graffiti began to appear on its old wooden timbers and doors, which had been sealed to travellers forever once *Last stop* had been announced for the very last time.

My neighbour, Romain, took one look at the graffiti on his first day of assigned community service at the station and figured it would take him about an hour to remove it. It didn't. It took half an hour. That left six months worth of Wednesdays on which to occupy himself until his obligation to the state was fulfilled.

Romain is a gardener, a man who has created magnificent gardens throughout the shire. Flower lovers lust after his prize dahlias and his landscaping is legendary. The Frenchman looked around and figured that the little neglected station could use a garden, something with vegetables for passers-by to eat and flowers for them to gaze upon and smell. Returning the following week with a spade and his box of tricks, he

began digging and was promptly joined by a Swiss gentleman who introduced himself as Urs. Urs, from Uki, also here to perform community service, was delighted to jump in and help and before noon the earth was cleared, tilled and ready for planting. It was time for lunch. Romain set up a small table and two chairs on the shady station platform and soon he and his workmate were tucking into a delicious Italian lunch bought at Mullum's Italian restaurant.

Catching sight of this charming and unexpected scene, I pulled up and joined them, just in time for coffee and cake from Scratch, the town's patisserie. So delightful was the experience, a bijou European restaurant lunch on a station platform, that I returned with a contribution the following week to find that a married couple from Germany had joined the lunchers. The table was now covered with a red-and-white checked cloth reminiscent of a café in the south of France. Yazmina, a French lady from the Caribbean who crochets the colourful hangings on the big tree at the town's roundabout, arrived on the scene, which was now a hotbed of discussion about world affairs and the EU in particular. The Wednesday lunches were beginning to resemble a meeting at the UN, only better. But the festivities were short-lived. Romain who works like a dog—although none I know—and expects others to keep up with him, cleared off the table and headed back to the garden. The first plants had taken hold, begun to grow and were enjoying their perfectly chosen spot behind the old building. Chillies, tomatoes, sugar cane, limes, pawpaws, avocados, pumpkins and every type of herb were lapping up the sunshine. I worried that bored kids might vandalise his garden after dark but Romain just

AIR BEE n'Be VACANCY

shrugged. Instead, he set about constructing a large bamboo seat where they could hang out and watch the moon and do whatever kids like to do on bamboo seats surrounded by a sweet-smelling garden.

On a recent visit back to the station, Romain was pleased to see that his garden, which has gone berserk, is being tended by someone who cares. His dahlias are about to bloom, and one day the avocado tree will start pumping out fruit to mix with the coriander and tomatoes and limes growing alongside to create a delicious guacamole. It will be time to break out the tortilla chips and set up the table again.

A Walk In The Rainforest

As my friend Karin heads off down the Amazon River, I content myself with a much easier trek—along the path from home and into the nearby rainforest. There will be no monkeys and probably no ayahuasca ceremonies but I will have zero jetlag and no nasty effects from a cocktail of inoculations. The rain is falling gently on my face as I hit the trail. The whip birds are cracking away so loudly that the little pademelon grazing on soft native ferns doesn't hear me coming. I have the joy of watching this red, pint-sized cousin of the kangaroo and wallaby nibble away until he suddenly gets a whiff of the intruder.

The pademelon—it's a bastardisation of an aboriginal word corrupted by the first settlers—is the lookout for the rainforest—the cockie. With a good thump of his short tail to warn fellow critters to be on their guard, bang, off he hops into the trees and disappears. The whip birds start up again somewhere high in the wet canopy. I crane my neck trying to see them, nearly getting whiplash, but you never see these elusive birds, so screw them. There is plenty else to see.

An echidna is snuffling in the leaves, head first, enjoying a big ant sandwich. The dog knows to ignore him and his weird spines, which are, in fact, modified hairs with fur between them for insulation. Mating season has ended and he's so over it. All that lining up nose to tail with other horny anteaters behind a single female hardly seemed worth it. At one stage he even dropped out and went off for a consoling ant lunch only to have

to join the back of the line later. When the lady was sick of the whole thing and ready to finally get it over with, the gentlemen dug a trench around her and proceeded to push each other in and out of it until the last man standing got to do the deed. Maybe he even considered just sneaking up on a hibernating female and surprising her with his bizarre four-pronged penis. Try sleeping through that.

The divine scent from the flowering cunjevoi lilies wafts from every side. There is a jungle of these mega toxic plants out there, some as tall as a person. Someone should capture that scent and bottle it. But good luck. This plant is one mean mother as I learned to my agony on encountering its burning sap. Strangely, it is the one antidote to the even-more-evil stinging tree that lurks nearby and which I have no intention of becoming acquainted with. But the candle-like flowers and huge elephant ears of the dreaded lily, shiny with rain, look harmless and wave at the wild raspberries growing all around. I tempt fate by greedily leaning across to pick a handful—less sweet than a traditional raspberry but delicious. At this time of year it's a treat for Scandinavian berry-loving friends to come and forage for them. Somewhere among the trees is a finger lime tree, the bush caviar, excellent with vodka. Frightened of a run-in with the giant stinging tree, I avoid seeking out this unique bush tucker and head on past that other—harmless—giant, the coolamon tree. Also known as the watermelon tree from the colour of its flowers, this is a remarkable and rare species. Strangely, in something called cauliflory—it blooms and fruits straight out of the trunk and branches, the flowers resembling velvety clumps of bright-rose or melon pink. When they flower, from November to February, birds come from afar to feast on the honey making the forest even noisier than usual.

The rain is starting to pelt down now and the creek is running fast. Somewhere down there is a platypus or two doing their thing. Given that these little oddballs spend 17 hours a day sleeping in their comfy riverbank dens, there is little to no hope of seeing them but it's exciting to know they're there. Nothing here to get the heart and adrenalin racing like an Amazon croc but beware! Who would expect this little recluse to be the only mammal capable of producing a toxin, from a venom gland in its spurs, no less?

Morphine doesn't even touch the sides of this particularly vicious and painful poison, and on the rare occasion that it has been inflicted—on fishermen and early explorers—the agony can last for weeks and even months and make a crocodile bite seem positively appealing. Recently scientists studying this amazing phenomenon have discovered that the toxin acts by stimulating electrical activity in the nerve cells that register pain and there is hope that this knowledge may hold the key to new treatments for chronic-pain sufferers. If I am ever fortunate enough to see a platypus, I will show it the deference it deserves.

DEWALT
Idle Hands
are the Devil's
Playthings

Do, Re, Me

Eric, a trained architect from San Francisco, and his French husband Pascal, a former industrial chemist, live beyond Kyogle with two pugs and a small herd of goats. Having discovered the joys of goat herding during a midlife crisis in the USA, Pascal chucked in corporate life and took up cheesemaking. The lifestyle suited, but annoying regulations stateside sent them looking for new pastures. Australia ended up the lucky beneficiary of these two talented fellows.

When not tending the goats and making delectable cheese, Pascal is a cheese consultant who flies around the country to teach eager students his secrets. Eric's considerable and personable talents are employed in community work as a volunteer at the Blue Knob Market, coordinating events. Lately he has been restoring old sewing machines; ones with crank handles and treadles. The type that requires no electricity and are thus increasingly in demand by those who sew in solar-powered homes, with no electricity to spare. These ornate old machines are things of beauty to work on and Eric has names for all fifteen he is currently restoring.

At night, with the small herd of goats asleep, Pascal picks up his needles and gets knitting, a hobby he took up to stop people on business-class flights talking to him in his earlier professional incarnation—it worked. While he constructs his intricate wool designs with multiple needles, Eric is busy with his embroidery needle.

Eric's infatuation with fine needlework was inspired by the

Sovereignty
Our Culture
Our Lands
Our Time
Police

POLICE

intriguing *Encyclopédie des Ouvrages de Dames* (*Encyclopedia of Ladies' Works*; by Therese de Dillmont, c. 1900) he happened upon as young boy. Poring over the delicious old techniques, styles and patterns, a love affair that would last a lifetime and cross a major ocean began. A pincushion on his sewing table reads *Follow Your Heart Even If It Takes You All The Way To Australia*.

Today, in the adopted country he has no intention of ever departing, Eric is a master embroiderer with serious ribbons to prove it. His first entry at the Sydney Royal Easter Show was a tablecloth featuring a map of Australia as its centrepiece, to commemorate his recently attained Australian citizenship. An honourable mention on that occasion was quickly followed by second place with a tea cosy, and finally, first place for his *Idle Hands are the Devil's Playthings*. Closer to home, he has triumphed at all the local shows, knitted with the Knitting Nannas on the frontlines of demos, and is a member of the Thursday Girl Quilting Circle.

His designs harken back to another era, celebrating the home when precious linens were passed down through the generations, not payWaved out of a Bed Bath N' Table. His latest creation is a marriage-equality sheet set. Embroidered across the top hem are the words *Equality Now* to match the *His* and *His* embroidered pillowcases. The centrepiece depicts the countries of the world that have approved marriage equality and the year they enacted it. Eric has been waiting, needle poised, to add Australia to the roll call. Luckily he has always been a man of great patience.

That patience was finally rewarded on 8 December 2017 when passage of the same-sex marriage act [properly, the *Marriage Amendment (Definition and Religious Freedoms) Act 2017*] brought

Australia into the modern age. As corks popped and streamers streamed across the land, Eric and Pascal, who had legally tied the knot abroad some years before, toasted their union as husband and husband for a second time. What the Royal Easter Show will make of Eric's commemorative needlework remains to be seen. I'm putting money on it being a show stopper.

Hair

When you look in the mirror and a tsunami-smashed bangalow palm stares back at you it's time to call Ron. Ron Snodgrass, beloved hairdresser to the women of the Northern Rivers, trucks up and down the motorways to rescue and revamp hair in the privacy of your own home. With his portable neck support to attach to any bathroom basin and trunksful of magic tricks, the arrival of this ex-Yarra Valley boy from the bush is always cause for celebration. A ripple of excitement zaps through the hills and dales as Ron's trusty SUV gets closer. Friends gather, Prosecco corks hit the bin and the music is amped up as the hairdressing party swings into action, like a bouncy shiny shampoo commercial. Even if your roots aren't screeching out for a touch up, there is always a temptation to turn up anyway, just to have the pleasure of this magician's company.

But forget weekends. Weekends are reserved for brides. Try getting between a bride and her hairdresser on the big day. You could end up in the A & E. Byron Bay is Destination Wedding—and big business, hauling huge sums of dosh into the shire each year. With wedding parties jetting in from all points north and south and from every country across the marriage-mad globe, Ron has seen it all—and survived to tell the tales. The good the bad and the ugly have all revealed their souls en route to the altar for there is probably no day as stressful and high-anxiety inducing as THE BIG DAY. It's not unusual for Ron to get emails from a semi-hysterical bride at 2 am the night before, making doubly sure he can give her beachy Byron

boho waves when her butt hits that chair in a few hours' time. Another email quickly follows. All the bridesmaids must have their hair up because, 'I want it all to be about me.'

Ron says they all want to look like the Kardashians, even Bruce now that he's Caitlyn, and if he hears, 'I want to look like a princess', one more time the normally gentle-hearted hairdresser might rip the hair right out of their head. Some brides, especially the short ones, go for the eternally popular beehive. 'The higher the hair, the closer to God, darling,' as one lady put it.

With anxiety going berserk, DIY brides can be prone to moods that only a bitch slap will take care of. But where are the bridesmaids when you need them? Getting pissed in the next room and nowhere in sight to squeeze her into the strapless sweetheart-neckline frock. The girls, especially new mummies, aren't passing up an occasion like this to let rip. The expressed milk is in the fridge and the kid has been slung across to the in-laws. It's party time.

By the time the cars roll up to deliver them to the venue they are so drunk and out of control that the sweat is running down their face, along with their makeup. And of course, it's started to rain. The battle-axe bride who by now everyone hates and are vowing never to speak to again, is heading in all her glory, resembling 'a fucking fridge,' into the car that will take her on her princess journey. 'You get the weather you deserve on your wedding day,' the make-up artist whispers to Ron as she hears Bridezilla scream one last order to her hapless ladies in waiting.

But at least they made it to the ceremony. On one memorable

occasion, after doing three hairstyles, with another eight still to go, Ron was informed that he had to go home. The bride had left. The marriage was off. And he wasn't getting paid.

On a happier occasion he was booked to do not one but two brides—soon to tie the knot with each other. In a house rented for the occasion, Ron set to work first upstairs with bride number one and her posse of bridesmaids before heading downstairs to do the same thing all over again with bride number two. When they finally emerged and stepped out of the door they were greeted by the whole street who had come out to watch the action. 'There must be two brothers getting married,' he heard an old lady squeal with delight as the two beauties and their entourages departed in separate cars. Sometimes, it's all worth it.

Lollypop Lollypop

For 15 years the most important woman in Mullumbimby was Sharon, the owner of the lolly shop, Mullumbimby Chocolates. Here, strategically located next to the ever-lively Lulu's café and close to the school, the lolly lady presided over all matters Mullum. Behind her counter, surrounded by jars of snakes and teeth, cobbers and frogs, stood the town's unofficial psychiatrist, private detective, nutritionist, cop and scientist. For there is an awful lot you can tell about children and the homes they come from by the lollies they buy, and don't buy, on their way to and from school. Why are they spending all their lunch money on pineapple chunks? Is there some pineapple chunk addicted standover merchant waiting for them in the playground? Are they lonely and trying to buy friends? Are they showing early signs of diabetes? Why have they NOT been in to make their regular purchase?

Nothing escaped the scrutiny of the lolly lady, who would make a quick phone call to the school or a child's parents. Every ingredient in the sweeties that could possibly affect her customers' health or behaviour was carefully considered before they were allowed to enter any little gob. She knew the chemical compounds and effects of all her products.

But above all, respect for her small customers and patience may have been her greatest qualities, for choosing the perfect bag of lollies can take a long time. One by one, she scooped them up and placed them in their little red-and-white-striped bag, never flustered when the customer changed their mind,

20¢
PINCH
30¢
RAINBOW
NERDS
3.00/100g
PIN
3
Choc

deciding at the last moment before their fifty cents ran out, against the sherbet and opting for a liquorice strap instead.

Not surprisingly, this saint was a very popular local. More than one little boy asked if she would like to marry their dad. Someone else enquired if she had a toilet because they would like to have their sleepover party in her shop. The strangest request came from a young woman who entered trailing two little kids—kids that she no longer wanted because she could no longer cope. The lolly lady assured her that she had come to exactly the right place and placed a call. The young mother walked out alone, sliding the door closed behind her.

Years after growing up, leaving school and moving away, kids return with their own children, or alone. I waited in line while a businessman in a suit—unusual here—carefully selected a bag of mixed lollies. Clearly he had more to spend than the average ten year-old but, nevertheless, he limited his selection to a few Minties, Redskins, bullets and clouds. As an afterthought, he added a Mega Boulder Jawbreaker, presumably to shove into some big-mouth irritant's cakehole at the meeting he was about to be late for if he changed his mind one more time.

You say you want a revolution

Just when you thought that the worst that could happen to you in Mullumbimby was another busker singing *Wind Beneath My Wings*, terrorists have rolled into town, the sound of their weapons sending fear through the streets. *Clickety-clack*—the Knitting Nannas Against Gas have struck again. They have brought their needles and are not afraid to use them. Today their target is the Commonwealth Bank. On the footpath outside, wearing their signature yellow knitted gear, these sisters in yarn are having a knit in. Settled in their portable chairs, flasks of tea at the ready, they are here to tell the world that the once-admired bank is funding one of the dirtiest environmental experiments in Australian history—the proposed Adani mine.

Galvanised by coal-seam-gas (CSG) fracking over the border on Queensland's Darling Downs, these uppity women from rural communities across the Northern Rivers first organised themselves into a collective with a purpose back in 2012. Without dropping a stitch, they determined to stop Big Mining in its tracks before it could thunder across the state to unleash its evil in NSW. Nose bleeds, ear bleeds, neurological damage to small children, chemical burns, ruined agricultural land, toxic water and threatened livelihoods were just some of the side effects of an incursion into rural communities by the Chinchilla-Tara CSG field in southern Queensland.

When energy giant Metgasco set the Northern Rivers in its sights for a massive gas fracking, the nannas grabbed their balls

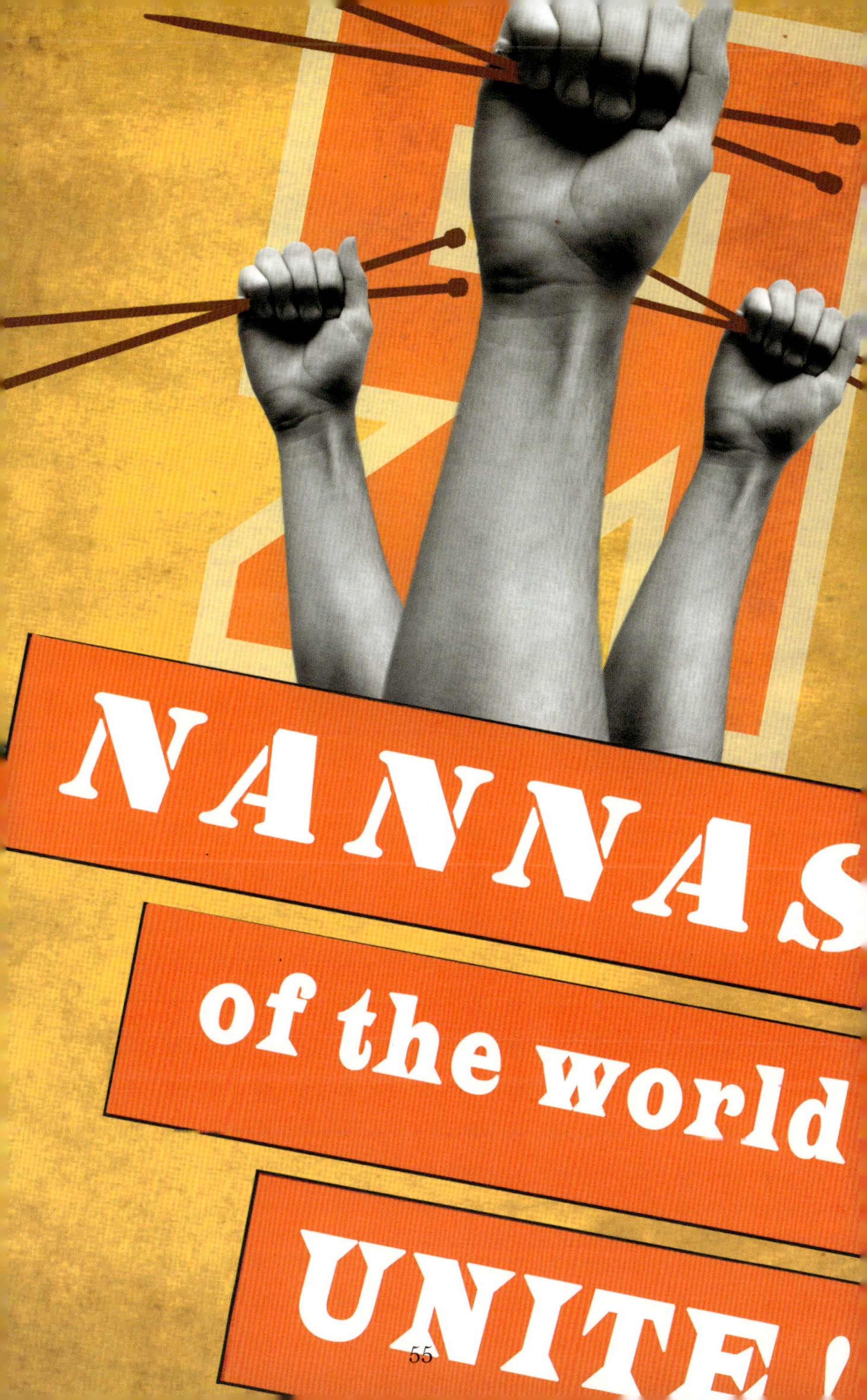
NANNAS
of the world
UNITE!

of wool and headed out to join the Lock the Gate Alliance at the coalface. Without a piercing or tattoo between them, they locked arms with hippies, ferals, and other non-National party folks—the type of people they wouldn't normally invite to tea.

As befitting country ladies, there is no violence or offensive behaviour. Their manifesto reads, 'We peacefully protest against the destruction of our land, air and water. We want to leave this land better than we found it ... We sit, knit, plot, have a yarn and a cuppa and bear witness to those who try to rape our land and divide our communities.'

The nannas stress that you do not have to be a nanna or even know how to cast on to sign up. Drawing on a long history of knitting used for non-violent political activism, they, 'view our knitting skills as less important than the act of bearing witness while we knit.'

What they bear witness to is a national disgrace that is spreading across the globe, anywhere where land can be raped to reap profits for greedy corporations and their cohorts, the politicians. There is now an international nanna alliance and ladies from the Northern Rivers are happy to share their experience and tips for nonviolent protest with sisters across the globe.

In solidarity with 'Lock the Gate' movement, they knit black-and-yellow triangles you see attached to properties throughout the region. Their needles are also busy knocking out long wool hangings to throw across gates of properties and roads that are about to be invaded by dastardly drilling rigs. And when the going gets tough and the ladies need to lock themselves to any heavy machinery trying to worm its ugly way onto a site, they will lock themselves onto it. When locking is necessary the nannas are prepared with, you guessed it, a knitted cushion and chain sleeves to prevent blisters. On boiling hot days, camped outside the offices of local politicians who dare to issue mining permits in their areas, the nannas are armed with eskies full of icy poles to give to anyone passing, cops included. The cops don't know how to handle the ladies, especially at the more frisky demonstrations. Who wants to be seen on YouTube stomping a granny?

The pollies duck and weave, embarrassed by a row of older ladies who are not going away until they get what they want. And get it they do. In March 2015, after months of protest at the Bentley site outside Lismore that on occasion turned nasty, gas company Metgasco announced that it was suspending its operations in the Northern Rivers due to community and shareholder pressure.

Across the world, from Fukushima to Ireland, the USA and Great Britain, the great nannahood is celebrating. As one lady eloquently put it, 'Take that you greedy, self-serving gasholes.'

Nannas of the world unite! You have nothing to lose but your chain stitch.

Miss Frisky is in the house

One Christmas I organised a fundraiser for my local dog-rescue centre. *Shout Your Dog a Selfie with Santa* was a joyous occasion. Every breed from Chihuahuas to Irish Wolfhounds bounded through the door of the picturesque Brunswick Picture House to cosy up with Santa in his big red suit and smile for the camera. No-one tried to pull off his beard or chew the decorations. Goodwill prevailed. At the end of the day, Santa's suit was slightly slobbered on and Santa himself needed more than a glass of milk but everyone went home with treats and happy snaps.

Most surprising was the number of young—and not so young—single men who fronted with their cherished hounds, most of which had been adopted. The adopters ranged from young, pale and sensitive with a Pit Bull-cross to big and boofy, plastered in tatts, with a Moodle. Some had made them special Christmas outfits that only a bloke could have come up with.

Just driving past The Brunswick Picture House with its stripy red-and-blue umbrellas and big red retro sign and light bulbs is guaranteed to lift any crappy mood you may be suffering. The building itself always looks as if it is smiling. So would you, if you had been sitting around neglected and miserable for two decades, the weather wreaking havoc on your once-good looks and natural charms.

The original Picture House opened its doors in 1952 and closed them again 30 years ago. Its future did not look bright until a pair of unlikely lads with a lot of heart fronted up with

BRUNSWIC
CAFE
COMEDY
BRUNSWICK PICT
ALL AGES SPECIAL
brunswickpicturehouse.com

PICTURE HOUSE
CIRCUS

enough money to rescue the old joint from the wreckers and begin a revamp. Energised by successful stints on Broadway and elsewhere of their popular cabaret show (winner of two Laurence Olivier awards and seen by over five-million people worldwide), Brett Haylock and Chris Chen wanted a mixed-arts venue to showcase live theatre, kids' shows, circus performances and classic films. After a long knockdown-drag-out fight with council, who wanted to close them down for some non-compliance at the behest of a yapping neighbour, overwhelming public support guaranteed that the show would go on.

Recently a *Bruns Goes Bollywood* celebration saw the locals and tourists turn up to enjoy live performances from the awesome Bollywood Sisters, henna designs in the pretty garden courtesy of friends at Henna Harem, and a special Indian menu of South Indian dosas, lassis and other delights. The main event was the Bollywood classic *Bride and Prejudice* and if that's not a good out night to you, you need to just stay home and go to bed.

I love their advertising:

TONIGHT! TONIGHT! TONIGHT!

Cheeky Cabaret is on! 7 pm. Start your Sat off right! So many acts. So much talent.
Don't worry about your job. Your upcoming birthday. Your car rego bills. The night is for fun: Miss Frisky is in the house!

Last night, an audience member mentioned, 'Oh my, she was amazing. Absolutely loved her!' Leave your troubles at the door. We'll look after you!'

The truth is … they sure will.

HOUSE

Doctor Doctor

Doctors in this neck of the woods are what you might call casual. The first time my very-English friend John went to see one, he was asked to take a seat in the waiting room until the doctor was ready. 'I'm free now, come on in', a voice finally announced. John looked around bemused. The only person in sight was a woman with wet slicked-back hair, wearing pants rolled up to her knees and sandy bare feet. The doctor was in. John, who comes from a long line of very proper English medicos who wouldn't be seen dead without a suit and tie, thought this was great.

To get to my last doctor you had to drive past fields of cows and pretty farming land until you reached a river that you crossed to enter a sort of jungle. The surgery had been built on stilts and was very rustic looking. Any minute you expected Tarzan to emerge and greet you. But it was just the doctor in a sarong. Where shall I tie the dog, I asked. 'Just bring him in,' he said as if I was some crazy person arriving for psychiatric help. So in we all went and were soon joined by the doctor's own dog. It was very cosy.

Home visits are even cosier. I love how the doc here still comes calling. It's one of the last holdouts of old-time civility and caring. Relatives have told me that in the old days in Ireland, doctors would arrive like visiting royalty in their coats and top hats. I'm not expecting to see a top (or any other) hat cross the threshold to my sickbed here in New South Wales anytime soon. But somehow it is reassuring to see that my GP is wearing shoes. Well, thongs anyway.

Sympathy for the devil

Little film societies thrive in the bush. On a wet Friday night I meet friends in an old Brunswick Heads church hall to watch The Third Man—for the sixth time. It costs $3 to get in. There is no heating so we rug up, wrapping ourselves in blankets. I took my own pink, fluffy hot-water bottle last winter, which everyone thought was a bit dorky—until the chill seeped up through the old gaping floorboards and they tried to steal it from under my wool throw.

First there is a short—featuring Harold Lloyd or the Marx Brothers, for example—followed by interval where delicious cakes and cookies are served with tea and coffee from big urns. It's like a church social without the preacher, although these are some pretty diehard movie buffs so much joy and reverence abounds.

My friends Katherine and Georgia who love any excuse to dress up in fancy costume are delighted when Indian director Satyajit Ray's beloved 1955 film Pather Panchali is to be shown and we are all encouraged to dress in theme. They arrive in swirling saris and salwar kameezes, their eyes rimmed with much kohl and red bindis painted between them. No-one else, including me, has bothered and they look a bit bonkers being the only fake Indians in the room.

Far from discouraged, they happily flash their bling and consider the dress-up possibilities for the up-coming Ninotchka starring Greta Garbo.

Sunday night is Russian movie night. Organised by a lovely

Russian woman who has recently moved here and is keen to share her cultural heritage, it is held in an upscale art gallery in Byron Bay.

We are greeted by Oxana, busy at work on her small portable stove cooking blinis and borscht. I feel like an enemy of the state when I announce to the assembled Russians that I hate borscht. They look at me as if I have vomited in front of the Queen. But it's good to air such blasphemies up front, otherwise you could end up having to eat the horrible stuff. I think of this as someone hands me one of Oxana's scrumptious pancakes that puts you in the perfect frame of mind for settling into the sixth episode of The Idiot.

Just as the BBC has dramatised all the best English classics starring their own company of top-drawer talent, the Russians have similarly been busy filming their own classic literature. The Master and Margarita—Mikhail Bulgakov's masterpiece—which, at one time, everyone read, has been turned into a stunning ten-part series. It is, hands down, one of the finest things I have ever seen.

Mikhail Bulgakov's novel features the devil, his talking cat and Margarita who travels the skies naked on a broomstick—definitely something on my bucket list. The novel is considered one of the masterpieces of 20th-century literature. The Rolling Stones based their hit Sympathy for the Devil on it.

If Margarita was to visit the Northern Rivers, she would no doubt swoop down for a flying visit to the CloudCatcher WitchCamp in the shadow of magical Mount Warning, which locals prefer to call by its traditional owners' name, Wollumbin.

Here in the 'exciting cauldrons for transformation' those looking to make magic, ritual and transformation part of their daily lives can come together for four magical nights' intensives.

We are not talking black magic here—more like activism or personal growth, and the word witch is gender non-specific. There are male witches and others who prefer to call themselves shamans, mediators, magicians, pagans, priestesses, elders, wise women, queers, feminists or radicals.

'Are you mad?', my Parisian neighbour Romain asks when I say I could sit through The Idiot a second time, which would make it 20-plus hours of Russian drama with subtitles. 'Why don't you just watch a good French film?'

What a good idea! A French film society. We can watch unbeatable old movies with Jean-Paul Belmondo and Alain Delon in Romain's living room. I can dress down in my pyjamas because with just one jump over the fence I'm home. I'll have to get him on to it but only if he can knock up a good French onion soup with his crêpes.

WELCOME TO
BYRON BAY
CHEER UP SLOWDOWN CHILL OUT

Pullets on parade (Million Chicken March)

Shove over Cate, Nicole and Kylie. You have some serious competition from a new Australian bird, a redhead whose major fashion statement is feathers. Her name is Little Miss Sunshine and she's a hen. As the star of the anti-battery-hen campaign *THAT AIN'T NO WAY TO TREAT A LADY*, the little chicken is popping up on screens and billboards across the world. This clever campaign from the wonderful Animals Australia aims to capitalise on consumers' increasing unease about the source of their eggs.

Nobody wants to think that the girl that laid them a perfect oval miracle for breakfast is tortured in a cage so tiny that she can never stretch her wings in her entire short life. And because poultry farmers are addicted to all those women's prison dramas on TV, they know only too well that caged girls love to fight. To nip this in the bud, the farmers slice off the ends of the poor old chickens' very sensitive beaks.

The hens on the property here are outside ladies. They waddle around the grounds raking at the earth for tasty things with their sharp claws. Then they have a nice old roll in the dust for a bath. Lots of squawking goes on because chooks are great communicators and each cluck means something different. They even cluck softly to their unborn chicks to teach them communication skills—and the chicks chirp right back from inside their shell.

Our girls' eggs are never fertilised because we don't have a

rooster. Roosters can have a bad rep as rapists and are a pain in the arse at dawn, so ours is a rooster-free zone. The girls' coop, to which they all trot back come dusk, is like a nunnery or some reality show where men are barred. It's spacious and cosy, with lovely fresh straw in the laying boxes. And do they lay?! Sometimes there are so many eggs—big beautiful bright-yellow-yokey eggs—that you don't know what to do with them. Visitors try to sneak away before you can bombard them with yet another couple of dozen and it gets so the whole neighbourhood is avoiding us. And still they spill out from the fridge and onto the benches in bowls that have been dated and colour coded.

If they want to lay eggs while out and about, they will find the oddest places to do it. The dog kennels are a favourite and so are the bags full of sheared alpaca wool. But old shoes and the seat of the tractor are handy too. You have to be careful where you sit down. Romain, my neighbour, found a hen on his bed recently. She was settled comfortably on top of the doona and had laid an egg. Now each day she lets herself into the house and makes a beeline for her new boudoir, clucking indignantly if he bars her from his bed. Reluctantly, she took up a position on the sofa to watch television. *The X Factor* (Australia) was playing. He couldn't quite grasp what she was clucking about but thought it had something to do with getting herself on the show. I reckon she'd be in with a chance. There've been a slew of acts on it but nobody has laid an egg yet. That takes real talent!

Turtles

If you wake up with an overwhelming urge to swim with a turtle and can't be fagged going all the way up to the Great Barrier Reef, a fine local alternative awaits. Byron Bay's Julian Rock Marine Reserve is a mere two-and-an half-kilometre boat ride from the shore, and a small flotilla of diving companies are lined up waiting to transport you to one of life's great and surreal experiences. Descending into this beautifully landscaped underwater garden you are going to meet some mind-bending locals among the lovely corals, colourful sponges, and wavering sea grasses.

Those 20 grey nurse sharks and their compadres, the spotted leopard sharks, surrounding you just look alarming. In fact, they are shy and docile, the bunny rabbits of the shark world, although I don't think I would try to have a smooch. They will mostly just ignore you, having more important and interesting things to do. Ditto for the big manta rays that glide through the water with their 300 useless little teeth, good for eating only plankton and other tiny things. These giants—*manta* is Spanish for blanket and manta rays do resemble large waving blankets—are seasonal visitors and only visit Julian Rocks at certain times of the year when the waters are right.

Turtles are there pretty much all the time. They have been cruising these waters for the past 10 million years and have seen it all. Even so, their curiosity remains and they will sometimes check you out if you are interesting.

Julian Rocks themselves were named in 1776 by Captain

WOW!

Cook (was anything not?) after his nephew and niece Juan and Julia back home in England. The captain himself never swam with the turtles or anything else. Apart from being far too busy dodging killer shoals, storms, marauding natives, and the exotic illnesses lurking to strike his crew at any moment, he could not swim. Had he got up close and personal with one of these gentle giants he would have realised that, far from being the dull old bloke who looks like he's heading home to change into slippers and a cardigan, the turtle is in actual fact quite a dude. Debate has raged in the scientific world as to how one should describe his genitalia—penis or phallus? *Schlong* might be the better word, for this guy is seriously hung.

The jury is still also out on why these appendages are so huge (up to half the length of his body) and why the otherwise humble turtle will suddenly let loose with an alarming display of his attributes. Neither mating nor defence seems to be the motive, for there needn't be a lady turtle or a rival in sight. Maybe, the marine biologists have concluded, he just does it to show off or because it's fun—something to put those giant Queensland gropers right off their game.

Roll another number for the road

It's marijuana patrol time again in the neighbourhood. The cops are out in their helicopters scouring the dense green vegetation for plantations of pot. It's hard to concentrate on working with a chopper kathumping overhead—quite literally. They fly so low that you expect them to land Santa-style on the roof any minute.

This is hippie country, famous for its weed, which grows like a weed. Stick anything in the ground here and it will sprout by lunchtime and be an old-growth forest by next week.

In the nearby village of Nimbin the annual MardiGrass is about to kick off. Coinciding with the start of harvesting season, the weekend-long blowout—and its more serious side—a drug-law-reform party—sees thousands of stoned locals and visitors from all over the world transform the sleepy little town into one big, happy, billowing bongathon.

Led most recently by a record 72-van konvoy of psychedelic DayGlo Kombi vans, a giant burning spliff is carried down the main street accompanied by a flotilla of floats, the Rolla Dooby Girls, and the Green Ganja Faeries who dance along spinning their magic. The Ganja Faeries work hard for months leading up to the festival rehearsing and sewing their flamboyant costumes. There is no age limit on fairyhood. It is a state of mind not body. The only requirements are a green tutu, a love of dancing and, of course, a fondness for Mother Nature's herb.

The weekend festivities include the Hemp Olympics featuring throwing and the tug o'peace with a hemp rope, natch. The bong

NEW SOU
POLICE

throw has male and female categories and the joint rolling has subdivisions. In a previous year, Bob the Joint Builder won the Speed Roll with a stunning 29-second time although Wendy, a local, wasn't far behind him and Andrea from Germany closely chased her. Wendy had her revenge in the Blindfold where she beat out Bob the Joint Builder and everyone else.

Entrants from Slovakia, Iran and France have duked it out in the Adverse Conditions event and the Artistic Roll, which was won by something called 'the helicopter.' At last year's MardiGrass highlights of the weekend included the wedding of Francis Moonshadow, Pot Poetry and Stoned Chess. Women with bare breasts painted in marijuana leaves mingled with old blokes in G-strings. Everyone was smiling—even some of the cops, when they weren't too busy busting people for possession of pot.

People fly, drive and hitch hike from all over the world to this tiny village to celebrate marijuana for medicinal and recreational uses in Australia. They groove to didgeridoo, saxophone, keys, African drums, rap and *doof-doof*. The aromas of a dozen different cuisines fight with the smell of the town's favourite herb and compete to attract customers with the munchies. The grand finale is of course the presentation of the Grower's Cup for best produce grown that year—although how the judges can possibly tell the difference by this stage is one of life's mysteries. Only the faeries know.

Turn Up The Music

A young woman who looks like rapper Iggy Azalea bounds past me on the climb up to the Byron lighthouse. Maybe it is Ms Azalea. She grew up in Mullumbimby and on a recent return here from her home in the USA tweeted, 'I've been in Australia for two hours and I've already eaten a sausage roll, a meat pie, 2 mini party pies, a Thai chicken curry pie & a lamington. I'm back bitches.' Amethyst Amelia Kelly started her singing career young, forming her first band at 14 and making her hip hop debut in Lismore. I'm guessing she also used to busk around the shire. Kids here start young, some really young, solo, or in little groups outside shops and cafes. Some are very good. Even if they're awful, people toss money into the hat. We encourage our local talent.

The latest musical sensation to put Mullum on the map is Dustyesky, the 28 man choir who started singing Russian folk songs for fun between vodkas, despite their inability to speak any Russian. Their first appearance was at the Mullumbimby Music festival some years ago, and they have recently played Womadelaide, where one reviewer raved about the 'sheer magnetism of their lusty masculinity.' Women love them. Men want to be them. The Motherland has discovered them. Putin is dreaming of a guest spot. Next stop, Moscow?

The festivals are growing, every year pulling in a bigger international crowd. Punters roll up, some in wet suits with a surf board under their arm. Bluesfest, Splendour in the Grass, Mullumbimby Music, Falls, Nimbin Blues and Roots. That's

the whole family sorted, from kids to grandpa. People who live near the Bluesfest site get free tickets for putting up with the annual invasion.

For years I resisted Bluesfest, never relishing the thought of a mud-crowd combo. I eventually caved in to go and see UB40, and had the added joy of the amazing Blind Boys of Alabama who have been singing together for seven decades. Their website says that their career 'has witnessed a World War, the civil rights movement, and the Summer of Love, the moon landing, Vietnam, and the fall of the Berlin Wall, JFK, MLK, and Malcolm X, the invention of the jukebox, the atomic bomb, and the internet.' Beat that Mick Jagger.

My friend Glenn has been faithfully making the pilgrimage from Melbourne to Byron each Easter weekend for years. I wanted to know how the festival has changed since he's been coming..... 'I first went to Byron Bay in 1994. It was for the then fledgling Blues and Roots Festival. Basically, it was like a bacchanal orgy on a huge mud heap. I loved it. For many years at Easter by road from Melbourne or by plane I went to the Festival. It just kept getting bigger and bigger and bigger as did the acts. From John Fogerty to Buddy Guy to watching REM in the pouring rain, it was a musical nirvana as well as a sort of wild orgy of sex, drugs, grog and food. However in 2015 I went to my last Festival. It was one of the best as it had returned to its roots. Smaller, more intimate and, above else, two amazing sets by Jon Mayall and The Bluesbreakers. You'd think I would be back with bells on the following year. Not so (and I don't wear bells although many festival goers do and that's about all they wear, especially many of the girls).

Accommodation had become too expensive, the festival moved away from its blues and roots - not for the first time - and over five days there were about two or three acts I wanted to see. Normally there'd be at least 10. And trudging through the mud and falling arse over tit had lost its charm. Funny how mud has its charm then it doesn't. It's just mud. Then I had what might be referred to as an epiphany of sorts. During the 20-odd years of boozing, grooving and various other guilty pleasures, I had never really discovered or even experienced the delights of Byron Bay central. So in 2016, I changed what I refer to as the "Byron Bay Experience" which it very much is. No more Easter festivals. Instead, a 17-day carnivale in late September with a clear plan. Music - nah. Great food, wine, cocktails, oysters - yeah. Essentially, to splash and splurge as much money on anything and everything my beating heart desired.....'

As for me, this year I'll be heading back to the tents. There will be rain and mud and there will be headliner Robert Plant. More enticingly, there will also be All Our Exes Live in Texas. The four-part indie folk girls first beguiled me at a local pub before their harmonies, mandolin, ukulele, accordion and guitar – combined with a lot of good looks, wit and charm won them an Aria, a tour of the USA with Midnight Oil and a soul-soaring, heart-melting album. Robert Plant once said, 'The female musicians I've met have been far more inspiring than the male ones. Women tend to be much more creative and ambitious. I think I may have been a woman in a past life.' Maybe the Exes will be feeling generous and invite him home to try out a few harmonies with that legendary falsetto voice.

I fought the law

Bangalow, the only intact Federation village on Australia's east coast, is one of the prettiest little country towns you will find anywhere. And if the developers and their fiendish plans don't get their way, it will remain so. Once home to dairy farmers and later to hippies and dairy farmers, the betting agency shared premises with the chemist. Today the main street is lined with trees and tasteful shopfronts sheltering under their old wooden verandahs. Although many of the old businesses have gone, those that remain include the local cop shop and lock-up.

When she first moved up here from Sydney, my friend Georgia had occasion to contact this small establishment. A prowler was lurking around the macadamia farm she was living on at Newrybar, some miles from Bangalow. When he answered her call, the police officer's ears, pricked up. They pricked up even more when she revealed her name and they checked their files; for this was a wanted woman; a danger to the state; a menace. The holder of three outstanding parking violations was a big catch for the Bangalow wallopers who were prepared to offer her a deal, pay up or do time—three nights in the local jail.

Georgia was packing her bag to head for incarceration when the sergeant in charge phoned to ask if she'd mind very much delaying her stay for a fortnight. She didn't mind at all, and two weeks later was ushered into her cell at the back of the old building where another convict soon joined her. This woman, also a parking villain, was the reason for the two-week delay.

SHM

...You had me at Hello
John Kaye

The cops were hoping to do both girls at once and they would be company for each other.

Now, locked away, leaving New South Wales a safer place, Georgia and her cellmate experienced life as convicts. This entailed having three good meals a day delivered to their door, much catch-up sleeping for the exhausted drug-counsellor cellmate and hours of uninterrupted reading and sunbathing in the yard for Georgia.

But, when enforced hard labour reared its ugly head, the ladies faced the awful reality that prison life was not all beer and skittles. Not only were they made to wash the cop car—twice—but they were also forced to move some firewood. When the pair was released after serving their time, the sergeant announced that they had done less work than any other prisoners ever held in the lockup. Now that's something to add to the résumé.

Down on the farm

If you have ever aspired to be a pig farmer but just didn't know where to begin, there is a workshop near Byron Bay with a loud oinking noise beckoning to you. The Pastured Pig Farming Workshops are held at The Farm, Byron shire's crowd-pleasing, family-friendly four-hectare working farm just outside Byron Bay. Here, set apart from the flourishing vegetable and flower beds, is a family (or two) of piglets happily chasing each other and rolling in the mud. It is an idyllic pig existence, 100% organic, biodynamic and sustainable, and is so, thanks to the guidance and expertise of Lee McCosker from PROOF—Pasture Raised On Open Fields. Since employing Ms McCosker's techniques which are taught in the aforementioned workshops, The Farm's pork production increased by more than 100% in 12 months.

I drag myself away from the frolicking piggies that will one day be reincarnated as lunch in the excellent Three Ducks restaurant on site, and head for a nearby field of sunflowers. Here, two teenage girls are taking selfies beside the giant smiley-faced flowers. They tell me they travel every season to see these magnificent blooms against the bright blue sky. This act of constancy is most apropos, for in mythology sunflowers are themselves symbols of constancy.

Back when Byron Bay was part of Gondwana and giant marsupials thudded across the land chomping their way through thick old forests, two water nymphs in another part of the world were both falling in love with the same bloke, the Greek god Apollo. Clytie and her sister Leucothea were naughty nymphs who broke all the rules. Each morning before dawn they danced blithely upon the riverbanks with all the other sprites, hastily descending to their watery world when the sun threatened to rise.

One morning, however, they decided to just hang on the bank to watch Apollo as he raced his golden chariot across the skies. And that's how the fight began. For when he smiled at them, both were immediately smitten. So smitten were they that Clytie dobbed her sister in to King Oceanus, who promptly locked her in a cave, leaving the way of true love open for the schemer. But no-one likes a treacherous nymph and Apollo was no exception. Each day as he passed her sitting up on the bank waiting for him, he turned the other way, concentrating on lighting the sky and nothing else. Bit by bit, heartbroken and now outlawed, Clytie grew thinner and thinner until her feet took root in the sand, her floaty frock became leaves and her face, still turned towards the sun—still hoping—became a sunflower.

Leaving the girls to the golden flowers, I return to the piglets, which now have a group of elderly folk gathered around watching them enjoy another good old roll in the mud.

'I wish I could go in there and have a wallow with them', an old lady with a walking frame announces. Her friends exchange looks indicating that she's done worse in her day. 'I wouldn't if I was you,' one advises. 'That fence is electrified.'

'In that case,' the Wild One replies, 'let's go and have another crème caramel. I'd give my good leg for one.'

On the road again

Many years ago a friend who is a bass player in a much-loved band was driving home one cold winter night on a lonely country road when he happened on an unusual sight. Beside a burning house stood a man in his underpants holding a small child by the hand. Sticking out of the man's chest was a pair of scissors.

A winding dark road at 3 am can do weird things to your mind but this was no hallucination, as he realised when he stopped and they got into his car. The man explained that an unknown assailant had attacked him and set fire to his house. His rescuer delivered him to the nearest hospital, left his details, and drove back off into what was now dawn.

Several weeks later he had a call from the cops who needed to see him. He had picked up a murderer who had killed his wife, he was now a witness in a homicide investigation. I am reminded of this recently as I head home up the mountain from town. She is standing by the side of the road dressed from head to toe in rich green velvet—including a hat that a lady might wear to a smart function. She has a matching bag over her shoulder and her thumb is stuck out at passing traffic. It is about 38 °C in the shade. I skid to a stop and roll down the window. 'Where are you going?', I ask and only then realise that the person is a man. He hops in and we climb the mountain to the next crossroads where I will drop him on his circuitous trip home to an outlying village. Someone, he assures me, will pick him up for the next leg. We are soon deep in chat about the

world going to the dogs and I am sorry to wave him goodbye. I am almost tempted to drive him all the way home, but it's quite far and the last time I did that I kind of regretted it. That time I had known it was a fella I was picking up. As it was another hot day and he wasn't going far from my place I offered to take him there.

All the way he regaled me with the story of his impending marriage on a beach and his grandmother who he was living with meanwhile. He did work around the property to help her out, his dear old gran. It all began to sound a little fishy, a little fabricated. The grandmother's house got further and further away than he had originally said. I began to wonder if I had picked up a murderer. Finally we rounded about the fiftieth bend along a bush road and he pointed to a house. We had arrived. I was so relieved I nearly kissed him. I didn't wait around to see if an old granny emerged from the somewhat crooked house—with or without scissors—and nearly skittled him as I reversed out of the driveway spitting gravel.

Everyone hitchhikes in these parts. Fuel is killingly expensive and the distances are long. I pick people up all the time. There has never been a problem other than some filthy sod wearing yoga pants that hadn't been washed since Buddha and who I almost had to disinfect the seat after. I've given rides recently to an Irish chakra student, an artist who paints the sacred sexual, a pastry chef, a street musician and his dog, and a young man so stoned I was terrified to let him out of the car. All the way up the mountain he drew circles in the air and laughed to himself. He was one of the most beautiful boys I have ever seen. In an area where angels are part of everyday life—much like next-door neighbours — he actually looked like one straight off the pages of my old Sunday School book, all golden and beatific. I wanted to warn him about being out on a lonely road alone and very off your head, at the mercy of strangers. But who am I to warn an angel?

'Didn't I pick you up hitchhiking a while ago?', I asked a man in a café recently. He looked at me as if I was a bit crazy and assured me that, 'Delightful as that would have been', he definitely hadn't been hitchhiking. A woman who must have been his wife shot me a filthy look as they climbed into a Mercedes. Come to think of it, that wouldn't be a bad pick-up line, at a pinch.

Dreadlock Holiday

Once upon a time in Brazil, I had been chatting to the Israeli hippie for quite some time before I noticed a tiny monkey emerging from his dreadlocks. It was wearing a string looped around its guardian's ear and both parties seemed to enjoy the arrangement. Since then I have always been on the lookout for other small creatures in dreadlocked heads, but the closest I have come is a story about a redback spider trying to make a nest in a young man's coils. The rest is pure mythology and urban legend.

Most dread wearers—and they are legion in the Rainbow Region—dedicate large amounts of time to their locks and a whole industry exists to nurture them. If you desire instant gratification and don't want to wait for them to grow, you can buy yourself some dreadlock extensions. Someone has taken the scissors—or a mattock—to their 'beautiful old set of dreadlocks' and is offering them for sale on a local website. All up there are 30 of these beauties—a snip at only $500. The seller will even attach them for you.

Erin of Isis Knot Dreadlocks on the Gold Coast has a steady stream of clients from Byron shire, Sydney and Melbourne—middle-aged women, tradies, 14-year-old boys. 'Not what you'd expect.' Her youngest client was three, the oldest closer to 70. Sometimes, she tells me, whole families will rock up seeking makeovers.

A *Wanted* ad on the Byron Bay Community Board has caught my attention. 'Hey everyone! I was wondering if anyone could help me with my dreadlock maintenance. I have a crochet hook but

PoP!
Woo
Hoo

need some help with my back dreadies. I can't offer any money because I'm on the bones of my arse ATM but I can offer great chats and lots of smiles and gratefulness. 😂'

Offers of help were quick to fly in and no doubt many smiles of gratitude were exchanged. Spiritual and existential matters may also have been discussed as dreading is much more than just a fashionable hairdo and has long historical form. Rastas kick started the modern-day western trend but, long before Bob Marley recruited the Wailers, babas and shamans, sadhus and nazarites went where others feared to dread. No-one knows for certain who had the first dreadies, although ancient Egyptian mummies have been uncovered with their locks still intact. Australian Aborigines and Native Americans also sported the matted look and young Masai warriors are recognised by their long, intricately braided hair coated in red ochre. By the time he is ready to become an elder, all this beautifully cultivated and maintained hair is shaved off by his mother and replaced by an ochre-dyed scalp.

Around the Northern Rivers there are very few ochre-dyed heads as yet. Mothers are not known to shave their son's heads to prepare them for a family life. They are too busy caring for their own locks.

The sound of silence

Audio archaeologists tell us that Henry VIII's England was one of the noisiest places in 16th-century Europe. Having decided that vigorous physical exercise was the duty of every Englishman, Henry issued a get-fit edict to his subjects. All men were expected to take turns ringing London's myriad bells—huge things sporting enormous thick ropes that one hung off, bouncing up and down to send their clanging across the length and breadth of London Town.

This din would have added to the onslaught of other noises—hooves and coach wheels on cobbled streets, town criers bellowing, traders shouting their wares, pissed fights and everyone shouting drunkenly at each other, for water was too foul to drink and strong ale was the chosen alternative.

In the hinterland of Byron Bay there are no pealing bells and very few town criers. The all-pervasive sound is silence—the deep and unrelenting silence of the tomb. Some people love it. It's the reason they come here, to get away from city noise. For them, the dawn chorus of the birds is quite enough audio stimulation for the day.

This cacophony, unlike anything else on earth, is probably not something Henry the Eighth himself could have abided after a long night on the grog. Promptly at 6 am, well before the first thin ribbon of light slinks across the sky, our feathered friends announce themselves to the new day. There are kookaburras, magpies, the bizarre catbirds, the show-off whip birds (pairs of them actually collaborate to create their unique whip-cracking

sound) and the melodious butcherbirds, to name a few. Just when you think they've all finally shut up and you can go back to sleep, the gigantic black-and-yellow cockatoos, not to be upstaged, arrive screeching to the pine trees. By then you are wide-awake and ready for some total silence with your cup of tea.

A friend, who has arrived, fried, from a gruelling job in New York, hoping for some of our famous quiet, has managed to sleep through this aural onslaught. Unfortunately, her visit has coincided with the annual shearing of the alpacas and its accompanying soundtrack, which brings to mind *The Silence of the Lambs*. I assure her that they are not being hurt, just carrying on, and will soon be back happily munching grass and spitting at each other, but she tells me it's worse than all the wailing cop car, ambulance and fire sirens on a Saturday night in Manhattan. I say I dream of sirens and loud horns honking, brakes screeching and music blasting out of doorways and cars. It's all very well—this total silence—if you're a holy man living in a cave but I, for one, like to hear some action even if it's the thudding of a *doof* echoing across the valley or the grunting and shrieking of a pair of koalas having loud sex now and then. Unless, of course, that's just the neighbours.

A kiss is just a kiss

My tech friend Big Fred has a big following of glamorous young women. Wherever you go with him in the shire, some young hottie is likely to bound out of a car and hurl herself into his arms. She will have done his hair or his nails or he will have done hers. Beauty tips will be exchanged and cosmetic surgeries discussed. Fred is an authority on breast implants and has experienced the occupational hazards (to himself) of a size too far.

A young lady had called him in to fix her keyboard. It kept putting spaces between the letters and the words by itself. Fred sat down at the desk and began typing. There were no extraneous spaces. It worked like a dream. But the next day she called him back and this time he took a brand-new keyboard with him. Again, he had no problem with any unwanted gaps appearing on the monitor. The third time the owner called, Fred made her sit and type, and the mystery was finally solved. Because of her short arms she was sitting very close to the desk, making her triple-D implants bounce and hit the keyboard. 'Her breasts nearly came out the length of her arms', he recalled. 'I call her Key Strokes.'

Fred's detective chops were called into service on another occasion when a different young lady was having trouble with her fax machine and specifically with a fax she was trying to send to her sister. The problem, she told Fred, was that despite what her husband said about putting the paper in at one end and it coming out the other, the paper was clearly still there after she had hit the send key. She was looking at it! Rapidly becoming fed up, he suggested she try sticking a stamp on it before sending—and she did. Next, Fred instructed her to write something that would make it uniquely hers and send it to his own personal machine. He would personally remove it from the tray, confirming that she was indeed successfully sending it.

To guarantee that it was from her and her alone, he suggested she put something of her very own on the paper. Indeed, how about a kiss? Duly, the paper with the big kissy lips arrived and he hurried across to show her and prove once and for all that she had sent a fax and it had arrived at the other end. She looked at the paper and up at Fred. 'That's not mine. That's black. My lipstick was pink.'

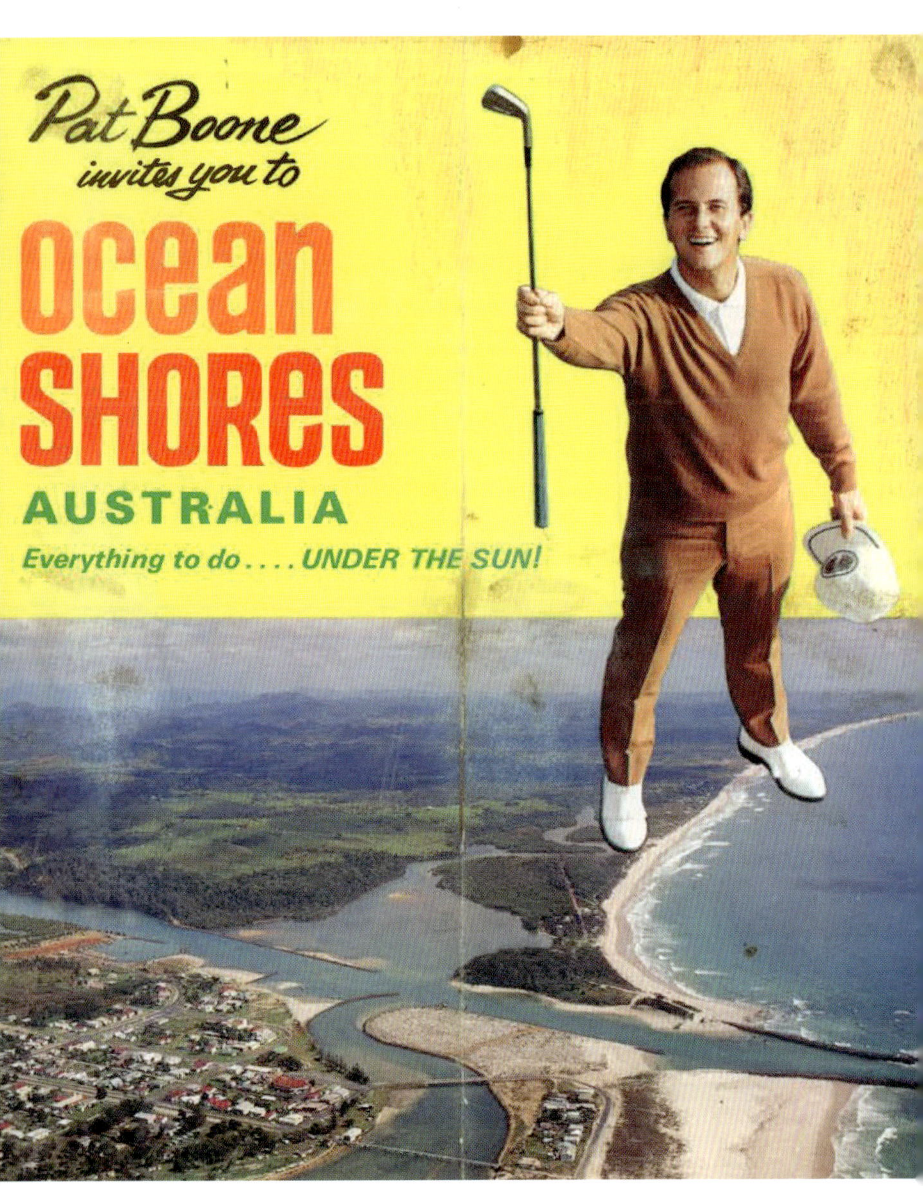
Pat Boone
invites you to
ocean
SHORES
AUSTRALIA
Everything to do . . . . UNDER THE SUN!

Pat Boone's
OCEAN SHORES

LAND, the true basis of all lasting wealth, cannot be made, or manufactured. The factory isn't making any more. Land is in limited supply, and land like **OCEAN SHORES** exists nowhere else. **OCEAN SHORES** is a wise investment. For the future — For your retirement — with a vacation wonderland as a BONUS.

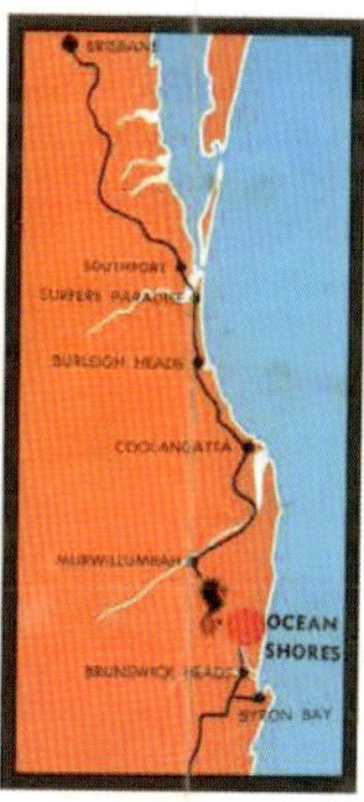

OCEAN SHORES is located on Pacific Coast Highway 1, one mile north of Brunswick Heads, 50 miles south of Surfers Paradise.

Pat Boone's
OCEAN SHORES

P.O. Box 19
Brunswick Heads N.S.W. 2483
Phone: 85 1308

Published for Ocean Shores by the
Summerland Tourist and Development Authority,
Box 472, P.O., Lismore, N.S.W.
Postcode 2480

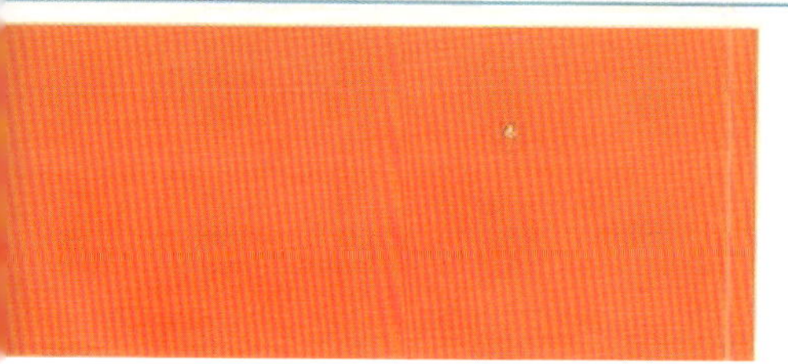

owned and developed by
Wendell-West Co. of Australia Pty. Ltd.
Suite No. 4201, Australia Square, Sydney, N.S.W. 2000

TWIN TOWNS PRINTERY

My caddie sings

When Clint rode into town, he hadn't come to shoot the joint up. Just to shoot some balls on the golf course. The year was 1966, and the newly completed Ocean Shores Golf Club was hosting a celebrity golf classic. Pat Boone, the conservative Christian crooner who was second only to Elvis in the charts and wet dreams of millions of girls was running the show, hoping to recoup some of the dosh he had sunk into the area's development. Billboard had ranked his big hit *Love Letters in the Sand* as the No. 2 song for 1957, and with a string of other hit songs and movies, Pat was flush. Along with his guest Clint Eastwood were baseball great Joe Namath and actor Fred MacMurray.

Ocean Shores has had a strange connection with fame and infamy since it reinvented itself in the early 1960s from sleepy farming land to a new development hotspot. Michael Hand, the fugitive US banker who vanished from Australia 35 years ago mired in the notorious Nugan Hand Bank scandal, had sharpened his teeth selling development lots up and down the Australian coast.

Pat Boone was an early investor in Hand's Ocean Shores Development, eventually losing everything. Later, Alan Bond took over the development and the stunningly beautiful Ocean Shores area started to take off. The golf course with just six holes opened in 1961, the year that Naval commander Alan Shepard Jr, America's first astronaut, was launched into space. Ten years later, now commander of Apollo 14, Shepard landed on the moon, whipped out a cleverly disguised makeshift six-iron, dropped two balls and took a swing, making him the only person to play golf anywhere other than planet earth. He was hoping that with reduced atmosphere and much lower gravity, his moon balls would travel much farther than his earthly ones, but this turned out not to be the case.

Meanwhile, back on the blue planet, Ocean Shores golfers were finally enjoying a nine-hole course. Sitting out on the balcony of the country club today, you could be forgiven for thinking that you had been transported to somewhere out of this world. With its eye-watering panoramic ocean views and laid-back reception areas, the club is a favourite for weddings. Now that the new marriage equality laws have been enacted, couples of all ilks can come here to celebrate their big day. Pat Boone would be disgusted. Virulently anti-homosexual, likening gay rights protests to terrorist attacks, the old Republican won't be writing any love letters in the sand, or anywhere else—some hate mail in a tweet, more likely.

Worms from hell

Having a morning coffee in one of the copious coffee shops that grace the streets of Mullumbimby, you might think you'd landed in the middle of a microbiology convention. But it would just be the locals comparing notes on their intestinal parasites. In Northern NSW where tank water is widely used, microscopic bugs have the power to inflict maximum anguish. The main offender is a tiny bugger called *Blastocystis hominis* that is extremely difficult, if not impossible, to get rid of. Most people in the area just manage it with Chinese wormwood, aka mugwort. But even the Chinese military would have their work cut out trying to wipe out this invader of the human gut.

In addition to powerful antibiotics or herbal remedies, depending on your bent, a super-strict diet must be observed. Best to prevent it infiltrating you in the first place. Water needs to be filtered, triple filtered and at the very least, boiled for half an hour before drinking. While sipping their kombucha around the table, other local exotic varieties of parasite are discussed in great detail (not for the faint-hearted at breakfast) and possible cures are pored over and dissected.

Antibiotics can only disarm the bugs if a pre antibiotic is taken to break down its walls to let the main drug do its job. Given a person may be the lucky carrier of up to 10 different species, getting rid of them is a full-time job. A friend has got all the local varieties plus an exotic one he apparently picked up in Thailand. It's called *Strongyloides*. Try saying that with an Australian accent. A biologist himself by profession, he is now an authority on the

SHEEP DIP
THE ORIGINAL OLDBURY
SHEEP DIP
MALT WHISKY
Woven from 16 single malt whiskies
70 cl e
Distilled & Bottled in Scotland
For The Spencerfield Spirit Co. Ltd. Spencerfield Farm
Inverkeithing Scotland Ky11 9la
40% vol

rotten things and ten years—and many courses of bizarre medications, including one imported from Ukraine, later—is starting to feel the last of them shooting through. As a final knockout punch, he is about to blast himself with that old farmer's friend—sheep drench.

I am relieved to hear he won't be hurling himself down a loading ramp into a trough of the powerful combined-fungicide-and-pesticide formula, just swallowing tablets specially formulated for humans. But if they don't work, it'll be straight into the trench.

That old hotel

When writer Bill Bryson was appearing at the Byron Writers Festival a few years ago, he asked to be rescued from the fray and taken on a sightseeing tour of the area. To his delight and hilarity, they arrived at the tiny town of Billinudgel where Bill propped himself up against the sign for a photo.

The name Billinudgel has long been attracting attention for one reason or another. No-one seems to know what it means. Is it Aboriginal, meaning perhaps *meeting of the waters* or *home of king parrots*? Why this would have been so, given the almost total absence of king parrots, will have to remain a mystery.

When the railway went in and the population soared—it was once put forward as a possible state capital—locals suggested renaming it Babynudgel. With the milky-sounding town of Mooball just up the road it could have been a cute, early tourist attraction.

Billinudgel was and is best known for its pub, a classic old wooden Aussie hotel owned and run for many years by the formidable Ma Ring, who had opened it in 1929 and reigned over the town from the saloon bar from 5 pm every day. Her name came from the parcels that would arrive by train addressed to her with her initials *MAR*, for Margaret Alice Ring.

During the war she played cards in the saloon with the Yanks of the 32nd Infantry Division, many of them

LAST of the
Mescalito
Mescalito
Mescalito

recovering from malaria, who were enjoying some R&R at nearby Camp Fingal Convalescent Camp up the road at Fingal Head. She always kept a handgun stashed in the drawer beside her.

Mrs Ring and her two friends, another lady publican and her sister, occasionally appeared together at the local races. The next day the newspaper would report a sighting of Mrs Dickie, Mrs Ring and Mrs Hole.

Ma lived to be 101, making her the oldest licensee in Australia. Politicians came calling. Bob Hawke got a lesson in how to pull a beer the proper way. The old photos line the walls today.

The railway has long gone and so have the US soldiers although the odd Vietnam vet will sometimes sit at the bar with the locals. What remains is a much-loved local watering hole with good music and good food. A 'schnitty and schooner' will cost you $15. You can enjoy them while watched over by Ma herself, glaring down from a painting above the bar. This tough old bird, who had zero tolerance for bad behaviour in her day, looks like she could still knock you off your barstool if you pissed off her bar staff, so don't try.

Tell 'em I'm surfin'

Hold it. Who are those exotic-looking gentlemen in the flashy shorts ploughing into the surf? Yep, it's the famous harmonic-chanting Gyuto Monks of Tibet. Even holy men need a day off and the Dalai Llama's personal choir is here to dig some ocean vibes. Based for years at a gompa (a Tibetan monastery or temple) near Bangalow, the usually robed harmonic chanters are pausing from their travels across the globe performing their unique deep-voice vocals, to have a dip. They've been visiting Australia for 25 years. They like Australia and Australia likes them.

The first time they ever clapped eyes on the ocean was at Umina Beach on New South Wales' Central Coast. Coming into contact with the salty water was an extraordinary experience for these mountain dwellers. They promptly lined up on the sand to chant a blessing, directed primarily at any lurking sharks. Their message to the man-eaters was simple—please respect the Buddhist principles of harmony.

I learn from a friend who used to drive the monks around and look out for them during their visits here, that as well as swimming and surfing they love to bicycle, to kick a ball around and to play cricket. They also love to op shop, with T-shirts high on their wish lists. All enjoy teaching Italian slang and eating a lot of chilli. Their mission is to help Buddhism achieve a higher profile and to raise funds for their monastery back home in Dharamsala, India, hometown to His Holiness in exile.

The monks come in groups of anything from five to 20, always accompanied by an elderly abbot. My friend says that the abbot he ferried around was obsessed with Inspector Rex, the German dog detective. The locals that flock to hear the extraordinary multi-phonic chanting of the Buddhist scriptures are happy to donate to help fund the monks' mission. Each group of visiting monks self-funds all their travel and accommodation expenses—sometimes they sleep in five-star hotels and other times on someone's floor.

In 2011 their *Pure Sounds* album, which resonates with spiritual power, was nominated for a Grammy Award and they have recorded in George Lucas's studio at Skywalker Ranch in California. These guys get around. They have played Glastonbury, chanted from the top of London's Shard, appeared in the Scottish Highlands and been welcomed to Aberdeen by the Lord Provost. The rock-star monks are pretty blasé about fame. They have higher matters on their minds. If I ever meet the abbot my friend described, I shall present him with an Inspector Rex T-shirt. After all, the German criminal-chasing police dog spent his whole life pursuing Buddhist principles of harmony.

Bring da beef

Sitting one day in a chic Cabo San Lucas restaurant overlooking Mexico's Sea of Cortez, we watched an American gentleman throw down his menu and beckon the waiter. 'Is the fish fresh?,' he barked.

'Of course, *señor*, it was caught this morning,' the waiter proclaimed, indicating the magnificent ocean spread before us, home to some of the world's most delectable seafood.

'Then gimme the beef burger.'

Some people just want their beef. Even here, deep in vegetarian country, the longing for red meat surprises me. Of course, it will have to be organic. Food here must also be gluten-free, dairy-free, fat-free, sugar-free, sulphur-free, sulphite-free, pesticide-free, preservative-free and triglyceride-free. Which can make choosing a restaurant a little time-consuming—unless you happen to be in the vicinity of a marvellous place called 20 000 Cows. This vegan restaurant with the 70s décor is in the rural town of Lismore, NSW. It was named after the number of cows' lives the owner figured he would save over the life of his establishment.

The kitchen makes my bathroom look like a football field and the wait is pretty long but when it comes, the food is sensational. With everything from spicy Yemeni stuffed pastry to creamy Malaysian curries (not made with real cream) it is always booked out.

I used to scoff at all this organic nonsense until friends who

Sexy Vegan
Sexy Vegan

were making a documentary about the takeover of the world's food supply by Big Business opened my foolish eyes. The bombarding of our food with chemicals and genetic modification (GM) is the stuff of horror movies. It is now being linked to the collapse of bee colonies across the planet and possibly to the astronomical spike in diseases like cancer and in brain disorders like autism and dementia. I like my honey and am quite attached to my brain so I am changing my ways. I have even started buying organic butter and milk. Pesticide-free vegetables are creeping into my shopping basket until the ones I've planted are ready to eat. But I've decided not to get too carried away. I have met people who are such strict vegans that they will only eat free-fall fruit. If the tree didn't give it up voluntarily they would rip off their own hand before ripping it from its source. They are called *extreme fruitarians*.

Visiting Mullumbimby, I am alone and can eat anything I want without lengthy consultation. I don't care what it's got in it. It's hard to beat a good old-fashioned Australian bakery. When you push open the flyscreen door the smell is overwhelmingly nostalgic and scrumptious.

I grab a gluten-full sausage roll with sugar-drenched tomato sauce and a sticky bun with pink icing full of preservatives and join a workman eating his pie and sauce on the bench outside. We nod at each other with mouths full of evil pastry. From the corner of my eye I see him take an apple turnover with cream out of a bag and ram it into his gob with fingers that look like bananas.

No doubt he had checked first that it was made from free-fall

MOO MOO CAFE
Thirsty?

Devil's bite

Apart from intestinal parasites, the other great scourge in these regions is the ubiquitous and hideous paralysis tick, which can produce unusual symptoms in animals and their owners. Once bitten some people succumb to full-on anaphylactic shock that, if they are lucky, necessitates urgent medical attention. Others develop a meat allergy several months after just one bite. The meats in question are pork, beef and lamb (and even whale). Fish and chicken are okay because they are not mammals. But even the humble marshmallow is unsafe if it contains beef gelatine.

Ticks love heat and moisture, both of which are found here in abundance. The ticks themselves so abound that people can and do make a living from collecting and selling them. The best way to do this is by dragging a light-coloured blanket, sheepskin or anything else the ghastly things will cling to, through tick country. Bring the tick trap home, pluck the ticks off it and sell them for antivenom. Vet-clinic counters have formaldehyde-filled jars in which you can view these bloated, engorged aliens that have been removed from furry patients. For some it is too late but every day the very existence of those dead ticks mean that the lives of other dogs and cats may have been saved. Most vets advise the use of expensive anti-tick and anti-flea medications but some pet owners do not wish to introduce strange chemicals into their animal's bloodstream, opting for vigilance instead. If you are lucky enough to spot the tick before it has ejected its toxins from its body and injected them into your pet, you can save them an unpleasant experience at the vet and yourself the unpleasant experience of footing the bill. The trick is to get a tick out in one fast swoop, disturbing it in the most minimal way before it can unleash its vileness into your hapless friend. Forget tweezers, the best way, we are told by people who know these things, is to have a bright light and a bottle of WART-Off at the ready. Ticks, like warts, have met their match with this potent (salicylic) acid. Give them a hit and watch them die.

Not quite so simple when you discover one embedded in your own head late on a Saturday night. Strategically located in a spot impossible to get at or even see—just feel—images of toxins leaking through the blood–brain barrier straight into your noggin has you diving for the WART-Off. But it's late and hard to aim right and somehow the entire contents of the bottle cascade down your neck and behind your ear like a mini chemical spill. You now have a nasty acid burn. When you finally stop squealing you are pretty sure that the weird sound emanating from your head is the tick having a laugh.

Mermaids

Kazzie Mahina is not the type of mermaid who lures men to their deaths in a watery grave. She is far too busy saving the ocean and its wildlife, and encouraging little girls (and their mummies) across the world to start exploring their own inner mermaid. After 15 years of hard work and determination, her dream to 'reshape the way women and ocean babies connect with the water' is finally catching on. The SSI, one of the world's largest diving companies is now offering an accredited mermaid course, and Mahina, with her shared commitment to preserving and promoting safe mermaiding, has been recruited as Ambassador for their Mermaid Program. 'The industry has finally caught up to my dreams for both kids and adults,' says Kazzie who - with her friend Hannah - is listed in Wikipedia as 'some of the first professional freelance mermaids appearing on the world scene around 2004.'

Once upon a time on a small beach on the south coast of NSW, a little girl with a big imagination and love of fantasy dreamed of joining the whales and dolphins that swam by. Tying her feet together with some old rope she taught herself to swim like a fish and listened to the waves whisper and roar, beckoning her in. Fast forward many years and the little mermaid, now a lovely blonde-tressed model - and her equally lovely blonde friend Hannah - are invited to swim with dolphins in Byron Bay for a community commercial about water awareness. The girls put their heads together and came up with tails – beautiful dolphin/mermaid tails that shimmered in the sun and swished through the water.

For the next year Mahina travelled solo around the world, learning to free dive in Thailand along the way. Enthralled little girls would watch her striding through airports, long hair swinging and tail slung across her shoulder, convinced they were seeing a real life mermaid, and Mahina would hand them a photo of herself slicing through the water like the mythical creature. She enjoyed spreading the magic. In Thailand this magic became a legend when amazed people watched her swimming the length of a beach under water. (It helps to have perfected a breath hold of 5.4 minutes.) 'They would say, 'I saw this girl with a tail and she didn't come up for air.' I never did let on. My code of conduct was never to let anyone see me put my tail on or off. '

The idea of becoming a professional mermaid was starting to take shape. All she needed was the perfect tail. Back home in Byron, with the help of special-effects artists, latex and silicone and an eye for beauty and functionality, this free spirit was soon ready to launch herself into the world as a pro. But the ability to slip in and out of your tail is just one of the requirements for life as a successful, professional mermaid. Others are experience as a free diver, strong swimming, and the talent to relax and appear glamourous in freezing cold water – as opposed to looking like a drowned rat. Mahina's background as a professional dancer in London, LA and Sydney, and her former life as a model and lifelong passion for extreme sports are all pivotal to this mermaid's success. When your work companions are dolphins, whales and sharks it also helps to have a deep affinity for the ocean and its creatures – and a whole lot of guts. 'I have always been an extreme sports girl,' she explains. 'When I was six months pregnant (with son Makoa Tide, now 5 years-old) I swam in a tank with sharks for a commercial. The water was freezing cold. I had zero visibility and I had to look like I was enjoying it.'

When she is not traveling to swim and dive for TV commercials, music video clips and photographic campaigns in exotic locations across the world, this former professional dancer, ski instructor and surfer hangs up her tails (she has three, all handmade by herself) in the home near Byron Bay she shares with her ecologist husband and two young sons. And it is from here that Kazzie runs her business, Mahina Mermaid, a mermaid brand and home to the famous and much loved Mahina MerFin.

The Mahina MerFin is the world's first ever mermaid flipper that this woman of many talents conceived and developed from scratch over six long crazy years. Made of recycled and natural rubber the eco fin was designed for performance, speed, and propulsion. The MerFins which are now currently being sold in over 80 nations around the globe, and are the holders of awards in the UK and USA, have given girls and women of all ages the chance to swish through the water looking and feeling like a mermaid.

And who wouldn't want to know what that feels like, even if you are nowhere near the ocean, and it's just you in your swimming pool in the backyard? Being a mermaid is a state of mind, after all. Or as Mahina would say, 'exhale and feel your 'being' mermaids.'

Morning, Mr Magpie

My friend Romain is in line at Divine Butchers in Mullumbimby when he recognises a tree worker ordering an expensive cut of sirloin steak. 'Nice dinner', Romain, a Frenchman who knows his meat, comments. 'It's not for me', the tree guy replies, 'It's for the magpies.'

Many people up here feed the magpies. They are persistent and very appealing with their morning visits and heavenly corralling. Heeding warnings that even our wildlife is getting fat—some too porky for take-off—people mostly feed them a few morsels of mince. But not this guy; from him they are getting an expensive steak. It is a peace offering.

Several days before, while driving 10 kilometres back to his campsite in the bush, the unfortunate fellow had hit a baby magpie and killed it. It was not his fault. The young, un-road savvy bird had scooted out in front of his wheel making a traumatic end to the day for both parties. But it was about to get a lot more traumatic. Some nights later—some very pitch-black bush nights later—the guy was tucked up asleep in his swag when retribution came pecking. Straight through the little mesh screen and right into his face.

An attack by a magpie is never a pleasant experience, especially at 4 am, woken out of a deep sleep, deep in the bush. It was swift and painful—just one nasty slash of that fearsome beak at his face. Did the parents pass the word along the road like the old bush telegraph or follow him themselves? Ten k's is nothing for a bird.

'Mincemeat would probably do the job just as well,' Romain suggests, looking at the expensive cut of meat. 'Yeah, maybe,' the fellow agrees. 'But they're not getting all of it. I'm keeping half for my own dinner.'

Nobody seems to know if his steak offering worked. Whether the magpies were mollified and called off the hit, cutting him a break—instead of a beak—because shortly afterwards the marked man left New South Wales and headed the hell back home. But word did get around that he had given up his swag and built himself a large box on the back of his truck to sleep in.

Magpies are known to swoop people who have annoyed them or their nests during nesting time. They have great memories and will target you when you are least expecting it. Back in Wilson's Creek, the question remains: Should the baby-magpie's killer have given its grieving family the whole steak?

Thank you for sending me an angel

The Archangel Mikael has been busy in the Northern Rivers. In January he appeared at a conference in Byron Bay on behalf of the United Planetary Nations from far-flung galaxies. Their message was simple and Mikael didn't beat around the bush. These brothers from other planets have been waiting aeons for the right moment to arrive in their starships—en masse—to convince we ignorant earthlings that we are not alone in the universe. When they come, earth will be a far greater place to live.

More recently, Mikael materialised in a Mullumbimby living room, using the body of a local lady, Valerie Barrow, to relay much the same message, as you can never hear it too often. We are a stupidly blind race and are forever doomed to nothingness until we listen to and absorb the wisdom of the brethren from afar. A million light years away from the Andromeda Galaxy, in Valerie's comfortable living room, locals have gathered to listen, prepared to have their hearts and minds opened to a universal truth.

Valerie, a dignified older lady, bows her head and waits for a spirit to enter her body. Her small audience watch as she emerges from a lively trance to inform them that the Archangel Mikael is among them. Nobody watching from the comfortable armchairs seems surprised to be in the presence of the leader of all angels and the army of God, one of the angels of the Apocalypse, no less. In his true angelic form Mikael is a tall young man, his blonde hair and golden eyes matching his golden cloak and tunic. In his right hand he carries a large sword.

But today he is manifesting in the earthly body of Valerie, clothed in a smart white tunic, her silver hair in harmonic convergence with a crystal necklace and earrings, no sword in sight. Mikael tells them that he is speaking for the Star people who come from the World of Light. These original beings wish to make a mass appearance to end conspiracy talk about whether they exist or not once and for all. Mikael goes on to say that they do indeed exist and have done so a lot longer than we have.

Star people have long walked among us. Some left to go home and others stayed. Was it they, perhaps, who constructed the famous Mullumbimby standing stones? This mysterious complex, known as Australia's Stonehenge, was once cited as the oldest temple in the world by Frederic Slater, then President of the Australian Archaeological Society. It contained, 'the basis of all knowledge in the beginning, now and to come.' Sadly, the farmer on whose land the stones stood, not one for knowledge, old or new, bulldozed the whole thing. So this is one less place for the Star people to make their appearance.

One day Mikael may clear up this local mystery, hopefully, before the hooves of the Four Horsemen of the Apocalypse's horses can be heard thundering towards town past the Bowlo.

Let's eat out

My friend Glenn Mitchell was back from Melbourne on his annual jaunt. A former restaurant columnist for a metropolitan paper, this man knows his food. Over a Sunday roast-lamb lunch we had cooked together (in what has become a yearly ritual) he filled me in on the local places at which he had been dining all week—the good the bad and the ugly.

'If there's one place to indulge gluttony it's Byron's amazing array of restaurants and bars. In 2016, I discovered probably the best restaurant in this glorious seaside retreat—the Orient Express—and it was purely by accident. I was on my way to the Bolthole—a truly great cocktail bar referred to by some of the younger locals as the Butthole (crazy kids). To my utter dismay, it was closed. Hmmmm, what to do at 9.30 on a quiet Tuesday night? That question was answered swiftly. Eat!!! Across the road, virtually next to the Beach Hotel was the Orient Express, an Asian-fusion place. Now I'm not usually a fan of fusion, be it food or music, particularly music. However, in for a penny, in for a pound, I thought.

It's a stunning restaurant befitting its name. You can dine outdoors but I chose a wonderfully marbled section indoors. Tastefully decorated, very friendly staff and to lob in just half an hour or so before closing I wasn't expecting a grand meal. Boy, was I wrong! Immaculate Chinese pancakes—essentially Peking duck—and possibly the most beautiful dish I have ever set my eyes on, the Thousand Island dumplings. Exquisite and washed down with a superb French white. Just after I ordered, I noticed about 30 or so crystal decanters in a glass cabinet above a bar. Being a crystal lover, I asked the waitress

whether they were for sale or just for show. Turned out they were Tippi, the owner's, favourites. Next thing I knew we were negotiating a price. I paid $250 for both and picked them up the next day beautifully wrapped and a lovely little card from the man himself. The following year, I mentioned to Tippi that I was the guy who bought the decanters. He remembered. 'Ah Glenn,' he said. 'I hope you put them to good use but no sale this year!'. Guess he had thought twice about the previous year. Lovely man and to be remembered by name was a genuine highlight of that particular trip.

It was the same when I went to Fishmongers, a great little seafood place. I walked in and the owner looked at me and said, 'Man, where you been?'. Having introduced him to a sensational Riesling—a Henschke, no less—the previous year, I handed him a couple of bottles of Pacifico, a REAL Mexican beer. Fishmongers is a must visit in Byron, especially for the grilled Australian king prawns and the calamari. One of the more off-the-track places is the Bowling Club. It has a superb bistro. I initially went there for a steak and got chatting to a guy who I thought was a kitchen hand. He assured me the steak was a ripper, however, he pointed out he'd recently had the pork cutlet with a pumpkin relish. He raved about it. 'It's new on the menu and we were just fooling around and came up with the relish. Couldn't believe that it worked,' he exclaimed.

That night I took his recommendation and it was everything he said it was and more. When I asked to speak to the chef, the same guy came out. Turned out he was the owner—lovely guy who'd cooked all around the world before retiring to Byron to 'run a little bistro'—one of Byron's best-kept secrets.

Naturally, Beach Hotel, sold yet again for $70 million, is a feature.

While the pub has lost its way somewhat, the views from the beer garden are as good as any in the world and across the road is Miss Margarita Mexican cantina. The cantina's happy hour with $11 margaritas and mojitos is an institution. However, I've never eaten there. It is pretty much house full every night of the week. But that's not the reason I've never dined there. When you've eaten U$2 burritos made by real Mexicans on a sidewalk in LA you're hardly going to pay $23 for a burrito in Byron Bay. Nor would you pay $3.75 an oyster at The Balcony, arguably Byron's best bar/restaurant. The thing is, you don't have to. Every Wednesday, The Balcony has an oyster happy hour. Delicious Sydney rock oysters at $1 a pop so I'll have two dozen, thanks. It's all a bit frantic as you might expect, however, the floor managers, particularly the delightful Danni, make sure it's not a mad free-for-all so the service stacks up very well, as do the oyster shells. It is a must, as are bookings Then we finish at the aforementioned Bolthole, which is appropriate as I always finished my night there. Located parallel to the main drag, as in a stumble down Beach Lane behind the Beach Hotel, it is a world-class cocktail bar. As good as any I've been to in New York, and there've been a few. Lazing in leather chesterfields and listening to the blues and the Rolling Stones, the guys and girls here are as friendly as can be. Always welcoming and having a laugh, the atmosphere is cool and bluesy. And the cocktails are outstanding. My personal favourite is the *Smoke and a Pancake*. It sets you back $19, however, it takes a good half-hour to drink. So I generally stay for about 90 minutes.

When I was last there, the delightful and vivacious Italian waitress greeted me with a hug every night while the owner-manager always came around from the bar to shake my hand. It didn't seem like business ploy; they seemed genuinely happy to see me.

That's what makes Byron so special. It's also why I'll probably never travel overseas again. Why would I when I have found paradise in the wonders of subtropical northern New South Wales?

Good grief

Traditionally held on All Hallows' Eve, the Day of the Dead celebration at the Crystal Castle has been postponed to a later date due to the rotten weather. Zenith Virago, the officiator, assures me that this will in no way inconvenience the dead. They have seen fire and rain and will come when they choose to. In fact, across the world and its many religions there are many days of the dead, even special days dedicated to the dead whose demise was caused by specific illnesses.

I shan't attempt to argue the point with a woman whose knowledge of dead souls far exceeds my own. For the past 20 years, Zenith, Byron's official Deathwalker, has been guiding and comforting the dying as they pass from life through the glass darkly and out the other side and their love ones too. She has facilitated 'death plans', given solace in final hours of life here on planet earth, and conducted funeral ceremonies for every sensitivity and creed. The much-loved local, who long ago left her native England, has no idea why she was singled out for such a calling, stopping at even calling it *a calling*. Her first foray into the funeral world was holding a ceremony for a beloved friend. Clearly she had a talent. Exuding compassion and strength, Zenith has become the confidant and comforter to so many.

With the rain stopped, the sun shining and the birds singing, a group of roughly 100 people has assembled for the reconvened Day of the Dead ceremony at the Crystal Castle. No-one speaks loudly; certainly there is no loud happy band. But, being Byron, there is some fancy dress, face paint and many bare feet. A choir can be heard rehearsing in the car park as mourners find seats on the grass or on chairs beyond the prayer wheels and stupas of this Buddhist sanctuary. Outside of heaven, it is surely the most tranquil place possible to honour the dearly departed. Zenith encourages us all to pin our messages and photos to the line strung behind her lectern—a fast-track to God—and to place the little handmade pottery offerings at its base. Children have been busy making these and adorning them with flowers at a special table. Zenith urges her congregation to be in their grief and to honour others'—let the person beside you weep, do not break into their private moment to try to comfort them.

We are gathered here, she tells us, to honour all of our losses, even the loss of relationships. Loss is loss. The choir opens the ceremony with an upbeat song but across the grassy gathering a swelling of grief is palpable. Some get up and leave. Zenith recognises people whose loved ones she has long-ago buried, people whose grief has shifted but not gone and never will. She reads a beautiful poem by Rumi, whose own funeral lasted 40 years, and the magpies chorus overhead. One by one the mourners go to the microphone and say aloud the name of their lost one. Some of the mourned are children. It is gut-wrenching and tears flow. Later, they will all walk down the path through the rainforest to place the notes and the little ceramics in the roots of a tree where they will rot and return to the earth from whence we all came.

I decide to skip this part. Sometimes sadness just wants its own company.

Snakes and ladders

One good thing about the rain is the absence of snakes. They tend to stay indoors, probably in bed. But you can't count on it. A neighbour told me he had even seen one in his compost pile in the dead of winter, with frost on its head.

A friend calls to drag me off to the beach for a dog walk. As an afterthought, she adds that she just found a snake skeleton and skin inside her bathroom. She thought it was just a python, harmless unless you are a small dog or cat or crocodile. A two-and-a-half-metre python ate a very large croc the other week; not around here, thankfully.

Our pythons don't usually get much longer than two metres and mostly they mind their own business. They eat the rats that eat the bananas, thereby enjoying a sort of rodent smoothie. When it's sunny they like to stretch out on tin rooves side by side like girls on the beach.

When they're not sun bathing or hunting, you can often hear them settling down for the night beneath the roof in your ceiling. A man I know was recently enjoying a quiet winter's evening beside the pot belly stove when he became aware of something trickling from above and landing on the top of the hot metal. The trickle quickly became a steady stream. As it hit the stove, a smell from hell began to penetrate his nostrils and those of the cat which promptly jumped down from the sofa and disappeared out the back door. The pong intensified until he too was fleeing outside, and returning to seal his bedroom door with tape before venturing beyond it to sleep.

Eventually, after leaving every door and window open to the elements for days to air the joint, the roof was removed and the mystery solved. A poor old python, one that had long resided happily and harmlessly in the ceiling close to the flue for warmth, had gone off to snake heaven, leaving its earthly remains to melt and ooze into the living room. 'What did it smell like?' I asked. 'Kind of gamey,' he explained. 'Dreadful, but not as bad as the other one that died above the kitchen and drizzled down into my cupboards, all through the food and plates and glasses. It had fully decomposed. The first one had just recently passed away and the heat had melted it.'

George the Snakeman, a colourful local character of European descent, has caught more than 3000 brown snakes, 300 red-bellied black snakes and smaller numbers of a variety of rarer species. Over the past 20 years his haul of these reviled reptiles has reached nearly 8000.

I first met George when I called him out to check on a large brown seen vanishing into an old shed near the house. He dropped to his knees and offered up a prayer of gratitude, 'On behalf of the snakes of the Northern Rivers, I would like to say thanks for giving us the perfect place to live'.

For a donation, George will go anywhere to catch a snake. You know it's him arriving because he has *SNAKEMAN* written across his truck—and in case you miss that and mistake him for the Avon lady, the word *SNAKEMAN* is also written twice on his big black leather boots in bold white letters, with the words intersecting to form a cross shape. In case you are in any doubt the back of the truck contains a large glass tank full of

writhing snakes.

To date, George has not been bitten by a brown. A red-bellied black, slithering across the road outside of Cheeky Monkey's nightclub in Byron and settling inside a car engine, gave him a nasty nip for his trouble. The cops helped to rush him to hospital and, after experiencing some wooziness and staying a while under observation, he was soon back in the saddle.

A few years ago our Snakeman was at war with a Melbourne businessman who had registered trade marks for 'snakeman' and 'snake man.' Fortunately, thanks to Section 124 of the federal *Trade Marks Act 1995*, which allows for 'prior use', the matter was resolved before it became too venomous. But it just goes to show that even snake catchers have to worry about possible trade-mark infringements.

PLEASE
NO
ROOSTER
DUMPING

Roadkill

A friend and his son are driving home in the dark on narrow, winding roads lined with potholes that are best avoided after nightfall. The moon is having a night off and there is no light coming from anywhere. The impenetrably dense canopy of trees adds to the scariness of the lonely road.

A wallaby leaps in front of the car and, mercifully, dies instantly from the impact. My friend, who is freaked out to have hit an animal, gets out to move the poor creature off the road. He and his boy are looking down at it remorsefully when a set of bright headlights appear, slow down and backlight the scene like an episode of *Fargo*.

The driver gets out and joins them looking down at the dead marsupial. 'Are you going to eat it?', he asks. 'Shall we eat it together?'

My friend is not the type to dine on roadkill. Indeed he cannot recall an occasion when he's been tempted. He had even declined the offer of some 'delicious squirrel' when visiting my neighbours in California.

Because there is a law against everything in Australia, eating dead native wildlife is highly illegal—unless you have a permit to do so. But this isn't what concerns him. He is too busy conjuring up the possibilities should he say yes. Would they skin and butcher it over a few beers before getting down to the serious business of butchering something else, something more closely resembling himself?

He never did find out. As the stranger bent down to examine his dinner, my friend and his son bolted for the car, pressed *LOCK* and sped off. In the morning when they passed the accident site the deceased wallaby was nowhere to be seen. Just a small bloodstain remained. Maybe the mystery motorist had recently read the wonderful *Roadkill recipes: A cookbook for visitors to Kangaroo Island* and fancied trying his hand at Skippy: The Bush Vindaloo. Or perhaps he was thinking of starting up his own roadkill café like the famous Route 66 stop in Arizona that features, among other tasty breakfast options, Flat Cat and Rigor-mortis Tortoise.

RoadKILL Café
you kill it, we grill it!!
Satay's
Sausage's
Kangaroo $ 2.00
Buffalo $ 2.00
Camel $ 2.00
Possum $ 2.00
Crocodile Ribs
Crocodile Thighs
Whitchetty Grubs
Possum
Wallaby Shanks
Mutton Bird

Here comes the rain again

Black cockatoos have screeched their way across the sky and people are getting excited. It's been an unusually long time of bone dry weather and everything is starting to suffer. Many locals believe that black cockies are harbingers of rain, and three flying in formation overhead are a sure-fire sign that the heavens will soon open, delivering salvation. So the sight of three huge black-and-yellow birds, each the size of a small drone, is cause for hope and celebration.

The alpacas in their paddock near the house are hissing and spitting at each other in what I can only assume is excitement too. All winter, all long, dry winter, that has reduced their paddock to dirt, they have been reliant on the mercy of humans, namely me, to feed them each day. If I am late they stand on the hill giving me some serious hairy eyeball through the kitchen window and guilt tripping me into leaving my breakfast and trudging up the hill to give them theirs.

These weird animals, hailing from South America, are camelids and thus related to camels and llamas. They started arriving in Australia in the late 1980s and for a while were all the rage. People keep them for their fleece, that softest of luxury wool of which rural gift shops seem particularly fond. Some people just want them as pets. They can be cuddly if they've been hand reared and you don't try to touch their heads—they hate that sensation. Early on in my feeding duties, I was rewarded for a quick head scratch with a nice gob of spit in the face—a particularly stinky gob of spit.

Some farmers put them to work guarding flocks of sheep and goats, particularly newborns, a job they apparently excel at. Who else do you have on the payroll that can see off foxes with a stare and chase them out of the paddock with an accompanying horror-movie soundtrack? And when that doesn't work, stomp them and crush their necks with great force? Lady alpacas are the hit men of the pack, although it is the males that are called 'macho.'

Lately, farming these animals for meat has begun to take off in Australia, surely an unnecessary development, surrounded as we are by every other kind of readily available flesh. More tender and adventurous alpaca owners harness up their pets and take them out visiting. They're a big hit at nursing homes and at anything to do with children.

A man and his alpaca that are about the same height, once wandered the streets of local towns attracting much attention. I used to lend my dog, a tried-and-tested chick magnet to single male friends to take on walks. But an alpaca is even more likely to get the girls stopping for a pat. I would have to remind the walkers about the head touching as a nice spit in the face would do nothing for getting a potential date off the starting blocks.

PHOTO CREDITS

Page

4 ©Romain Vallet

6 ©Asa Mark

8 ©Asa Mark

11 ©Ron Snodgrass

12-13 ©Brian Reichman

14 ©Valerie Morton

15 ©Valerie Morton

16-17 ©Romain Vallet

18 ©Che

21 Maximilian Paradiz

23 ©Valerie Morton

24-25 ©Valerie Morton

27 ©Asa Mark

29 ©Valerie Morton

31 ©Valerie Morton

32 ©Asa Mark

35 ©Asa Mark

36 ©Eric Smith

38-39 ©Marie Cameron

43 ©Madphoto.com.au

45 ©Madphoto.com.au

46 ©Rachel Stone. (Food by Anthea Amore :Organic Passion Catering)

49 ©Irina Tennant

50 ©Asa Mark

52-53 ©Irina Tennant

59 ©Melody London

60-61 ©Valerie Morton

63 ©Julie Kantor

64-65 ©Erin London

69 MGM

70 ©Asa Mark

71 ©Valerie Morton

73 ©Romain Vallet

75 ©Romain Vallet

76-77 ©Irina Tennant

79 Brocken Inaglory

83 ©Nimbin Ganja Faeries

84 ©Isis Knot Dreadlocks

87 ©Karin Escombe-wolhuter

89 ©Karin Escombe-wolhuter

91 Laura Murray

93 ©Valerie Morton

94 ©Valerie Morton

96 ©Valerie Morton

99 ©Valerie Morton

101 ©Valerie Morton

105 ©Isis Knot Dreadlocks

106 ©Isis Knot Dreadlocks

109 ©Asa Mark

110-111 ©Irina Tennant

112-113 ©Irina Tennant

114-115 ©Brunswick Valley Historical Society

119 ©Valerie Morton

123-124 ©Billinudgel Hotel

129-129 ©Irina Tennant

131 ©Valerie Morton

133 Zpunout

134-135 ©Valerie Morton

137 ©Thor Englestad

141 Jarrah Tree

142-143 ©Irina Tennant

147 Andromeda by NASA

149-150 ©Jerry Burke (Free Man Skateboarding)

153 ©Erin London

154 ©Irina Tennant

157 ©Irina Tennant

158 ©Brunswick Valley Historical Society

160 ©Asa Mark

162 ©Asa Mark

164 ©Asa Mark

167 ChildofMidnight

169-170 ©Romain Vallet

174 ©Julie Kantor

Valerie Morton is a writer and film maker who has called Byron Shire home for the past 12 years. She currently lives in a rainforest where the day can start with a cane toad in a gumboot and end with a magic mushroom–fuelled doof echoing across the valley.